ENGAGING *Creative* THINKING:

Activities to Integrate Creative Problem Solving

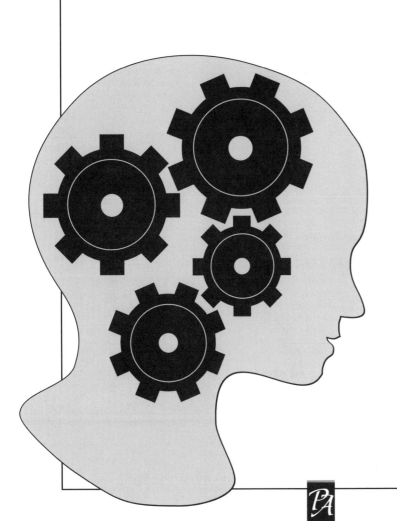

BERTIE KINGORE
AUTHOR

Jeffery Kingore
GRAPHIC DESIGN

PROFESSIONAL ASSOCIATES PUBLISHING
www.kingore.com

Current Publications by

Bertie Kingore, Ph.D.

Alphabetters: Thinking Adventures with the Alphabet (Task cards)
Assessment: Time Saving Procedures for Busy Teachers, 2nd ed.
Integrating Thinking: Practical Strategies and Activities to Encourage High-Level Responses
Just What I Need! Learning Experiences to Use on Multiple Days in Multiple Ways
Kingore Observation Inventory (KOI), 2nd ed.
Literature Celebrations: Catalysts for High-Level Book Responses, 2nd ed.
Portfolios: Enriching and Assessing All Students; Identifying the Gifted, Grades K-6
Reading Strategies for Advanced Primary Readers
Reading Strategies for Advanced Primary Readers: Professional Development Guide
Rubrics and More! The Assessment Companion (CD-ROM included)
Teaching Without Nonsense: Activities to Encourage High-Level Responses
We Care: A Curriculum for Preschool Through Kindergarten, 2nd ed.

FOR INFORMATION OR ORDERS CONTACT:

PROFESSIONAL ASSOCIATES PUBLISHING
PO Box 28056
Austin, Texas 78755-8056
Toll free phone/fax: 866-335-1460

ENGAGING CREATIVE THINKING:
Activities to Integrate Creative Problem Solving

Grades K through 12

Copyright © 1998 Bertie Kingore
4th printing, 2003

Published by **PROFESSIONAL ASSOCIATES PUBLISHING**

Printed in the United States of America
ISBN: 0-9657911-2-2

TABLE OF CONTENTS

INTRODUCTION

As students move into upper grade levels, the number and kinds of creative projects typically decrease. Often, schools are too busy covering the content to indulge in creative, hands-on activities, yet students of all ages learn and retain information best when they are more actively involved at high levels of thinking. Furthermore, diverse learning styles and multiple intelligences demand learning experiences beyond traditional paper and pencil tasks. The challenge is how to incorporate appropriate content and skills into creative learning opportunities for students.

Engaging Creative Thinking: Activities to Integrate Creative Problem Solving encourages productive thinking and problem solving in language arts, math, science, and social studies for students in kindergarten through high school. This book demonstrates:

- How creative problem solving can integrate basic skills in multiple content areas.

- The use of creative problem solving to increase students' high-level thinking.

- Experiences that increase students' learning while minimizing teacher preparation.

- Learning tasks that motivate students to excel.

- Activities that increase students' responsibility and active involvement in learning.

- Guidelines and structures for developing additional divergent tasks that allow teachers to implement creative problem solving within their units of study.

These learning experiences are not just something to do on Friday afternoon to provide fun for your students. Rather, the intent is to share strategies you can use often to help you teach more effectively.

MODELING THE IMPORTANCE OF CREATIVE PROBLEM SOLVING

Remind your students of the real-life application of creative problem solving by showing a brief clip from the movie Apollo 13 (1995). Focus on the scenes after the Apollo crew's survival problems are known. "Houston, we have a problem." They must literally fit a square peg into a round hole by adapting items in their spacecraft. Discuss how creative solutions often involve using the familiar in unfamiliar ways.

Kingore, B. (1998). Engaging Creative Thinking. Austin: Professional Associates Publishing

THE CREATIVE PROBLEM SOLVING PROCESS ——————

The creative problem-solving steps presented here are based on the original work of Osborn (1963) and Parnes (1981). Their model has evolved over the years with modifications from several theorists including Isaksen and Treffinger (1985). This adaptation is designed to describe the creative process and to enable educators to implement creative problem solving more effectively in classroom learning situations.

In step one, Problem Awareness, the problem is noted. It is followed by Fact Finding in which relevant information is gathered. Use investigative words such as how, why, who, when, what, and where to help focus this collection of facts and opinions. Problem Finding is the third step. It is crucial to define the problem in open-ended statements instead of narrow confines. Thus, IWWMW ("In what ways might we...") or IWWMI (In what ways might I...) is the preferred format for stating problems. The classic problem of trying to create a better mouse trap has more solution options if restated: "In what ways might we get rid of the rodents." After stating the problem in different ways, select one statement to concentrate on for the rest of the problem solving process. In Idea Finding, the fourth step, the objective is to generate several possible solutions to the selected problem. The fifth step is Solution Finding with the goal of determining the best solution from the previously generated ideas. The Decision-Making Grid on page 7 is an effective technique to assist in prioritizing solutions during this step. In the sixth step, Acceptance Finding, formulate a plan with a step-by-step sequence to implement the solution. Visual-spatial students may develop a flow chart to detail this step. The final step, Implementation and Rethinking, invites students to execute their plan in writing and then reflect upon changes they could make.

While the seven steps work together to expedite the problem-solving process, fewer steps can be used when deemed more appropriate for the situation. At times, teachers may want to focus on only one or two steps for a particular context.

Kingore, B. (1998). Engaging Creative Thinking. Austin: Professional Associates Publishing

sTEPS IN THE CREATIVE PROBLEM-SOLVING PROCESS

BEGIN...

1. PROBLEM AWARENESS
Be alert to the problem.

2. FACT FINDING
Gather as much information as possible.

3. PROBLEM FINDING
Define the problem in open-ended statements.
"IWWMW"

4. IDEA FINDING
Think of several possible solutions.

5. SOLUTION FINDING
Reach a decision by determining
the best solution.

6. ACCEPTANCE FINDING
Action plan: Think of ways to gain acceptance of
your plan. Write the best procedure and sequence
for carrying out your plan.

7. IMPLEMENTATION AND RETHINKING
What would you do differently?

Kingore, B. (1998). <u>Engaging Creative Thinking</u>. Austin: Professional Associates Publishing

CREATIVE PROBLEM SOLVING WITH LITERATURE

Literature offers excellent opportunities to implement creative problem solving. The form for Problem Solving with Literature on the following pages guides students through the problem-solving process with step-by-step prompts. Students can respond to problems in a story by developing their ideas for possible solutions. While the task can be completed by individuals, a small group collaborating on a solution often produces a richer experience. Students working together to brainstorm multiple possibilities may respond with a wider variety of ideas than an individual might produce alone.

A bibliography of quality literature is included, featuring books that pose problems applicable to the creative problem-solving process. The teacher or students read to a specific point in the story where the problem is revealed. At that point, stop reading, and use the Problem Solving with Literature forms to determine the best solution for that situation. After completing the solution, students read the rest of the book.

One observed benefit of this process is the students' curiosity regarding how their solution compares with the author's. After completing their problem solving, most students are eager to finish reading the book and learn the author's solution. Consider using comparative techniques such as a Venn diagram or concept webbing when discussing similarities and differences between the students' and author's versions.

Two completed students examples are provided as models of the process. The Lon Po Po example on page 9 shows the problem solving of primary students after listening to their teacher read aloud the first part of this book by Ed Young. She then guided them through the problem-solving steps and recorded their ideas. The second example on page 11 is used with Karen Cushman's novel, Catherine, Called Birdie, in a ninth grade classroom. To motivate students to read and analyze the story, the teacher initially read selected passages of the book. Then, the students worked in small groups to brainstorm ideas. The groups collaborated by sharing ideas, completing the problem-solving grid, and creating an action plan. After everyone read the novel, a lively discussion ensued comparing their problem solving with the author's solution.

Kingore, B. (1998). Engaging Creative Thinking. Austin: Professional Associates Publishing

BOOKS FOR CREATIVE PROBLEM SOLVING

ESPECIALLY FOR YOUNG STUDENTS

Allard, Harry. (1977). <u>Miss Nelson is Missing!</u> Boston: Houghton Mifflin.

Brumbeau, Jeff. (2000). <u>The Quiltmaker's Gift</u>. Dublin, MN: Pfeifer-Hamilton.

Bunting, Eve. (1994). <u>Smokey Night</u>. New York: Harcourt Brace Jovanovich.

DePaola, Tomie. (1978). <u>Pancakes for Breakfast</u>. New York: Harcourt Brace Jovanovich.

Jones, Rebecca C. (1991). <u>Matthew and Tilly</u>. New York: Trumpet Club.

Maynard, Bill. (1997). <u>Incredible Ned</u>. New York: Putnam's Sons.

McCully, Emily Arnold. (1992). <u>Mirette on the High Wire</u>. New York: Putnam.

Mendez, Phil. (1989). <u>The Black Snowman</u>. New York: Scholastic.

Most, Bernard. (1990). <u>The Cow That Went Oink</u>. New York: Scholastic.

Pfister, Marcus. (1992). <u>The Rainbow Fish</u>. New York: North-South Books.

Pilkey, Dav. (1994). <u>Dog Breath: The Horrible Trouble With Hally Tosis</u>. New York: The Blue Sky Press.

Rylant, Cynthia. (1985). <u>The Relatives Came</u>. New York: Scholastic.

Say, Allen. (1993). <u>Grandfather's Journey</u>. Boston: Houghton Mifflin.

Stanley, Diane. (1997). <u>Rumpelstiltskin's Daughter</u>. New York: Morrow.

Waber, Bernard. (1972). <u>Ira Sleeps Over</u>. Boston: Houghton Mifflin.

Young, Ed. (1989). <u>Lon Po Po</u>. New York: Philomel.

ESPECIALLY FOR OLDER STUDENTS

Bloor, Edward. (1997). <u>Tangerine</u>. New York: Harcourt Brace.

Cushman, Karen. (1994). <u>Catherine, Called Birdy</u>. New York: Harper Collins.

Deedy, Carmen Agra. (1991). <u>Agatha's Feather Bed: Not Just Another Wild Goose Story</u>. Atlanta: Peachtree.

Holman, Felice. (1974). <u>Slake's Limbo</u>. New York: Scholastic.

Konigsberg, E. L. (1996). <u>View from Saturday</u>. New York: Atheneum.

Lowry, Lois. (1993). <u>The Giver</u>. Boston: Houghton Mifflin.

Martin, Rafe. (1992). <u>The Rough-Faced Girl</u>. New York: Scholastic.

Naylor, Phyllis Reynolds. (1992). <u>Shiloh</u>. New York: Atheneum.

Paterson, Katherine. (1994). <u>The Flip-Flop Girl</u>. New York: Trumpet Club.

Paulsen, Gary. (1987). <u>Hatchet</u>. New York: Trumpet Club.

Paulsen, Gary. (1996). <u>Brian's Winter</u>. New York: Delacorte.

Polacco, Patricia. (1992). <u>Chicken Sunday</u>. New York: Scholastic.

Polacco, Patricia. (1994). <u>Pink and Say</u>. New York: Philomel.

Sacher, Louis. (1998). <u>Holes</u>. Ney York: Farrar, Straus, & Giroux.

Schwartz, David. (1989). <u>If You Made a Million</u>. New York: Scholastic.

Spinelli, Jerry. (1990). <u>Maniac Magee</u>. New York: Scholastic.

Voigt, Cynthia. (1981). <u>Homecoming</u>. New York: Fawcett Juniper.

Wynne-Jones, Tim. (1996). <u>The Maestro</u>. New York: Orchard.

Kingore, B. (1998). <u>Engaging Creative Thinking</u>. Austin: Professional Associates Publishing

PROBLEM SOLVING WITH LITERATURE

NAME _____   DATE _____

TOPIC OR BOOK _____

Problem Awareness
STEP 1

WHAT IS WRONG?

_____

_____

_____

_____

Fact Finding
STEP 2

WHAT ARE THE FACTS?

Who? _____

What? _____

When? _____

Where? _____

How? _____

Why? _____

Problem Finding
STEP 3

DEFINE THE PROBLEM.
Use the facts to develop several open-ended problem statements. Put a check (✓) beside your best idea.

1.   In what ways might I/we _____

_____

_____?

2.   In what ways might I/we _____

_____?

3.   In what ways might I/we _____

_____?

4.   In what ways might I/we _____

_____?

Kingore, B. (1998). Engaging Creative Thinking. Austin: Professional Associates Publishing

THINK OF IDEAS.

Brainstorm several possible ways in which the problem you checked in Step 3 can be solved. Stick to the facts, but think freely and imaginatively. List your ideas.

1. _____

_____

_____

2. _____

_____

_____

3. _____

_____

4. _____

_____

5. _____

_____

6. _____

_____

7. _____

_____

_____

DECISION MAKING: DETERMINING THE BEST SOLUTION

On the next page, list four relevant criteria to help evaluate the solutions. Then, list your five best ideas from Step 4. Use the following scale to score the potential effectiveness of each idea for each criterion.

EXCELLENT   5 ◄—— 4 —— 3 —— 2 ——► 1   POOR

Check (✓) the solution with the highest total points.

Kingore, B. (1998). <u>Engaging Creative Thinking</u>. Austin: Professional Associates Publishing

Decision-Making Grid

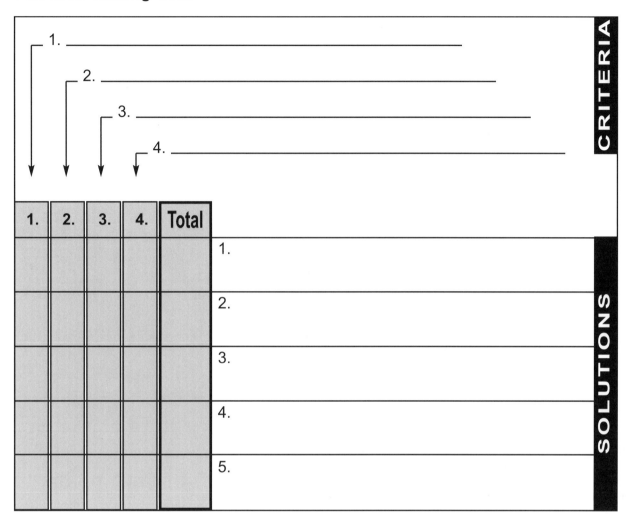

1. _____

2. _____

3. _____

4. _____

CRITERIA

1.	2.	3.	4.	Total	
					1.
					2.
					3.
					4.
					5.

SOLUTIONS

Acceptance Finding

STEP 6

ACTION PLAN

Think of ways to gain acceptance of your plan. Consider the best procedure and sequence to carry out your plan, and then write it out step-by-step.

1. _____
   _____

2. _____
   _____

3. _____
   _____

Kingore, B. (1998). <u>Engaging Creative Thinking</u>. Austin: Professional Associates Publishing

4. _____

_____

5. _____

_____

6. _____

_____

7. _____

_____

8. _____

_____

IMPLEMENTATION: PUTTING YOUR PLAN TO WORK
Try out your plan and describe how well it works.

Implementation
and Rethinking

STEP 7

_____

_____

_____

_____

_____

_____

_____

_____

RETHINKING
What would you do differently?

It's *great* to
solve a problem!

_____

_____

_____

_____

_____

_____

Kingore, B. (1998). Engaging Creative Thinking. Austin: Professional Associates Publishing

THINK OF IDEAS.

Brainstorm several possible ways in which the problem you checked in Step 3 can be solved. Stick to the facts, but think freely and imaginatively. List your ideas.

Idea Finding

STEP 4

1. *Two girls could get the wolf's attention while the other girl runs for help.*

2. *They could use their bedspread in the house and pull it over themselves to look like a big monster and scare him away.*

3. *They could tie him up and run to safety.*

4. *They could play a game like hide and go seek with him and lose him on purpose.*

5. *They could run outside and lock him in the house.*

6. *They could use food to distract him and run away as he eats.*

7. _____

DECISION MAKING: DETERMINING THE BEST SOLUTION

On the next page, list four relevant criteria to help evaluate the solutions. Then, list your five best ideas from Step 4. Use the following scale to score the potential effectiveness of each idea for each criterion.

Solution Finding

STEP 5

EXCELLENT 5 ←→ 4 —— 3 —— 2 ←→ 1 POOR

Check (✓) the solution with the highest total points.

Kingore, B. (1998). <u>Engaging Creative Thinking</u>. Austin: Professional Associates Publishing

LON PO PO -- PAGE 2

PROBLEM SOLVING WITH LITERATURE

NAME *Ms. Wilhelm's second grade class* DATE *January 29*

TOPIC OR BOOK *Lon Po Po by Ed Young*

Problem Awareness

STEP 1

WHAT IS WRONG?

The wolf is trying to get the girls!

Fact Finding

STEP 2

WHAT ARE THE FACTS?

Who? *Shang, Tao, Paotze*

What? *trapped by the wolf*

When? *on their grandmother's birthday*

Where? *their home in the country*

How? *the wolf persuades the girls to let him in*

Why? *the wolf pretends to be Po Po*

Problem Finding

STEP 3

DEFINE THE PROBLEM.

Use the facts to develop several open-ended problem statements. Put a check (✓) beside your best idea.

1. In what ways might I/we *figure out sooner who the wolf really is* ?

2. In what ways might I/we *get mother back to help us* ?

3. ✓ In what ways might I/we *escape from the wolf* ?

4. In what ways might I/we *get rid of the wolf* ?

Kingore, B. (1998). <u>Engaging Creative Thinking</u>. Austin: Professional Associates Publishing

LON PO PO -- PAGE 1

Kingore, B. (1998). <u>Engaging Creative Thinking</u>. Austin: Professional Associates Publishing

LON PO PO -- PAGE 4

4. The girls play closer to the house while he is farther away.
5. They let him be "it" a lot.
6. When the wolf is "it" and counting to one million, the girls run to the house and lose him.
7. They lock the door and never let him in again.
8.

IMPLEMENTATION: PUTTING YOUR PLAN TO WORK
Try out your plan and describe how well it works.

The plan worked great. The girls played several rounds of hide and seek to gain the wolf's trust. When he was really starting to enjoy himself, they let him be "it". While he was hiding far away and counting, they got in. They locked him out and never opened the door again until their mother got home.

STEP 7 — Implementation and Rethinking

It's great to solve a problem!

RETHINKING
What would you do differently?

Next time, the girls should give all the game players a cap to wear and make the wolf's bright red to see him easily.
Next time, don't be fooled by strangers.
If you don't let him in, you don't have a problem!

Kingore, B. (1998). Engaging Creative Thinking. Austin: Professional Associates Publishing

---

LON PO PO -- PAGE 3

Decision-Making Grid

CRITERIA
1. Keep the girls safe
2. Not hurt the wolf badly
3. Something they can really do
4. Uses materials they have

SOLUTIONS

	1.	2.	3.	4.	Total
1. One girl runs for help.	1	5	2	5	13
2. Use food to distract him and run away as he eats.	1	5	2	3	11
3. Act like a monster and scare him away.	1	5	1	5	12
4. Tie him up, and run to safety.	1	4	1	3	9
5. Play a game like hide and seek and "lose" him.	2	5	4	5	(16)

ACTION PLAN
Think of ways to gain acceptance of your plan. Consider the best procedure and sequence to carry out your plan, and then write it out step-by-step.

1. *The girls remind themselves how to play hide and seek.*
2. *They tell the wolf they want to play with him to make him feel happy.*
3. *They play after dark so it is harder for him to see.*

STEP 6 — Acceptance Finding

Kingore, B. (1998). Engaging Creative Thinking. Austin: Professional Associates Publishing

PROBLEM SOLVING WITH LITERATURE

NAME **Ms. Preizer's ninth grade class**   DATE **March 7**

TOPIC OR BOOK **Catherine, Called Birdy by Karen Cushman**

STEP 1 — Problem Awareness

WHAT IS WRONG?

Catherine is in conflict with her father.

STEP 2 — Fact Finding

WHAT ARE THE FACTS?

Who? **Catherine**

What? **She is being forced into marriage.**

When? **1290**

Where? **Stonebridge Village, England**

How? **her father's strong will: her wit and spunk**

Why? **She is trapped by the time's conventions.**

STEP 3 — Problem Finding

DEFINE THE PROBLEM.
Use the facts to develop several open-ended problem statements. Put a check (✓) beside your best idea.

1. In what ways might ~~we~~ **she overcome the obstacles of being a female in the medieval culture** ?

2. In what ways might ~~we~~ **she manage to choose her own husband** ?

✓ 3. In what ways might ~~we~~ **she guide her own destiny**

4. In what ways might ~~we~~ **she experience life outside her village** ?

Kingore, B. (1998). Engaging Creative Thinking. Austin: Professional Associates Publishing

CATHERINE, CALLED BIRDY -- PAGE 1

THINK OF IDEAS.
Brainstorm several possible ways in which the problem you checked in Step 3 can be solved. Stick to the facts, but think freely and imaginatively. List your ideas.

STEP 4 — Idea Finding

1. **She could join a nunnery and not have to marry anyone.**

2. **She could openly defy her father and refuse to marry.**

3. **She could succumb to her father's wishes and resign to her lot in life.**

4. **She could masquerade the rest of her life as a male and control her own life.**

5. **Edward could help her escape and assume a new identity.**

6. **She could attempt to reason with her father.**

7. **She could marry a weak but very compassionate man she could manipulate and control to satisfy her interests.**

STEP 5 — Solution Finding

DECISION MAKING: DETERMINING THE BEST SOLUTION
On the next page, list four relevant criteria to help evaluate the solutions. Then, list your five best ideas from Step 4. Use the following scale to score the potential effectiveness of each idea for each criterion.

EXCELLENT   5 —— 4 —— 3 —— 2 —— 1   POOR

Check (✓) the solution with the highest total points.

Kingore, B. (1998). Engaging Creative Thinking. Austin: Professional Associates Publishing

CATHERINE, CALLED BIRDY -- PAGE 2

4. Catherine will tell her father the qualities most important to her in a husband.
5. She will concede to her father the final approval or disapproval of her choice.
6.
7.
8.

IMPLEMENTATION: PUTTING YOUR PLAN TO WORK
Try out your plan and describe how well it works.

Catherine talked with her father, and he listened, compromising somewhat. He allowed some travel with a chaperon, and she was taught some things not usually available to women. However, he didn't allow her to choose her suitor until later when her charm finally won him over.

Implementation and Rethinking — STEP 7

RETHINKING
What would you do differently?

It would be interesting to pursue the idea of Catherine masquerading as a boy and develop the adventures she would experience.

It's great to solve a problem!

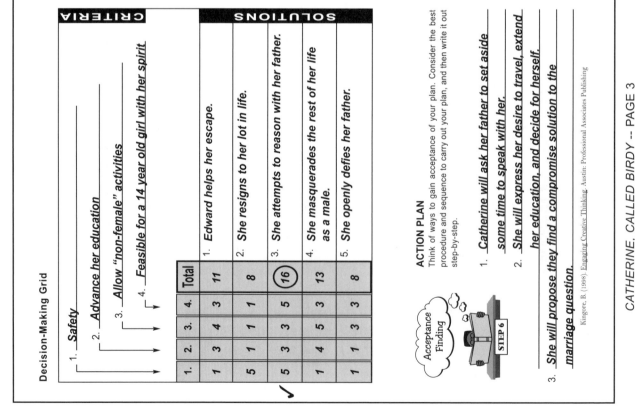

Decision-Making Grid

CRITERIA
1. Safety
2. Advance her education
3. Allow "non-female" activities
4. Feasible for a 14 year old girl with her spirit

SOLUTIONS
1. Edward helps her escape.
2. She resigns to her lot in life.
3. She attempts to reason with her father.
4. She masquerades the rest of her life as a male.
5. She openly defies her father.

	1.	2.	3.	4.	Total
1.	1	3	4	3	11
2.	5	1	1	1	8
3.	5	3	3	5	(16)
4.	1	4	5	3	13
5.	1	3	3	1	8

ACTION PLAN
Think of ways to gain acceptance of your plan. Consider the best procedure and sequence to carry out your plan, and then write it out step-by-step.

Acceptance Finding — STEP 6

1. Catherine will ask her father to set aside some time to speak with her.
2. She will express her desire to travel, extend her education, and decide for herself.
3. She will propose they find a compromise solution to the marriage question.

CREATIVE PROBLEM-SOLVING PERFORMANCE TASKS

Creative problem-solving performance tasks actively engage students in demonstrating their thinking and skill mastery. Students enjoy these enticing experiences and are highly motivated to excel. They implement many of the problem-solving steps as they work together to complete each task.

These tasks have been successfully used with kindergarten through high school students in mixed-ability classrooms. Because of their open-ended nature, these problems encourage students' diversity in learning styles and talents. All students can complete these tasks, but their solutions demonstrate very different degrees of complexity, depth of information, and sophistication.

Five performance tasks incorporating multiple content skills in language arts, math, science, and social studies are provided. Each task also serves as a model for developing your own creative problem-solving tasks.

These performance tasks are presented in an elaborated form to integrate extensive learning experiences. Teachers who prefer less complexity or a shorter time involvement can easily simplify any of these problem-solving tasks by eliminating some of the criteria and/or some of the steps in the process.

GUIDELINES

CREATIVE PROBLEM-SOLVING PERFORMANCE TASKS NEED TO BE CONTENT-DRIVEN AND INCORPORATE SIGNIFICANT LEARNING OPPORTUNITIES.

Problem-solving tasks are performance assignments that integrate multiple skills in an active learning format. Avoid using or developing problems that may be fun and entertaining but do not result in significant learning. Instead, think about the specific concepts and skills that could be applied through a creative problem-solving task and plan problems that incorporate several learning proficiencies.

Kingore, B. (1998). <u>Engaging Creative Thinking</u>. Austin: Professional Associates Publishing

It is important to analyze your rationale and objectives for the task and to communicate those objectives to students in advance of the project. "This is why we are going to..." Also, consider corresponding with parents to inform them of the learning potential.

Problem-solving tasks encourage learning proficiencies, such as:

- **Motivating students to want to excel;**
- **Reinforcing communication and collaboration skills;**
- **Encouraging decision making;**
- **Encouraging time management ;**
- **Incorporating problem solving and critical-thinking skills;**
- **Applying organizational skills and responsibility;**
- **Allowing students to formulate questions and test solutions;**
- **Reinforcing interpersonal skills; and**
- **Incorporating content area concepts and skills;**

PROBLEM-SOLVING PERFORMANCE TASKS PROVIDE SUCCESSFUL AND VALID LEARNING EXPERIENCES WHEN THEY INCORPORATE THE FOLLOWING COMPONENTS.

- **High-level thinking is promoted.**
  Open-ended problems take the top off of tasks so participants can operate at higher levels. Students continually analyze and synthesize as they work to construct creative solutions.

- **Multiple intelligences and learning styles are incorporated.**
  The subparts and open-ended nature of each task provides many ways for different styles and intelligences to be validated.

- **Complexity and challenge are encouraged.**
  The tasks involve varying levels of difficulty and incorporate appropriate levels of challenge to account for individual readiness levels.

- **Students are encouraged to become producers, not to remain consumers.**
  Since more than one correct answer is possible, students construct their own solutions rather than simply reinvent ours. Students literally produce that which did not exist before they completed the task.

Kingore, B. (1998). <u>Engaging Creative Thinking</u>. Austin: Professional Associates Publishing

NOTES

- **Student choice is supported.**
  Students choose which roles to assume in each task and select from an array of extensions to enhance their learning.

- **Content integration is promoted.**
  The learning experiences allow students to connect prior knowledge and new information rather than stress isolated skills. These performance tasks are designed to encourage the application of skills across the curriculum.

- **Active involvement is required.**
  Students minds and bodies are actively engaged in each task.

- **Criteria for success are shared.**
  Clearly established criteria are communicated to the students in advance of the task and used for self or collaborative evaluation. Examples of criteria incorporated in the problems include: complexity of solution, accuracy and depth of information, quality, group cooperation, evidence of understanding, appearance, originality, integration of skills, organization, time management, construction, technology, and presentation.

IMPLEMENTING PERFORMANCE TASKS

ADMINISTRATION AND MANAGEMENT

1. Share criteria and evaluation forms with students before beginning a problem-solving task. Students aim higher when they clearly understand what is expected.

2. Announce to students: "You may use anything you hear from another group." That idea encourages each group to work quietly among themselves so others do not hear and copy their strategies.

3. Minimize teacher preparation time. Constantly analyze what students should be doing for themselves.

4. Each group is responsible for cleaning the area in which they are working. The task is not officially completed until the area is clean and reorganized.

5. Those who complete the task early are encouraged to select an extension activity from the suggestions provided. These activities are related to the original problem and pose extended challenge and involvement.

6. Use creative problem-solving tasks as activities for centers. The group of students working at the center collaborates to complete the problem.

SKILL INTEGRATION

1. Develop lists of concepts and skills in multiple content areas that you want students to incorporate as they work toward solutions. Then, organize the problem-solving task to maximize those learning opportunities.

2. Compile your own concepts and skills lists or adapt the lists included with each problem. When you have an appropriate list, laminate and post it for visitors to read. That list helps others understand the educational value of what otherwise may seem to be frivolous.

3. Discuss the concepts and skills with students so they understand the intent of the task.

4. Require students to self-evaluate at the completion of a task and assess their levels of achievement. The self-evaluations may be completed through discussions or written responses. Each problem includes one or more evaluation examples to guide students' thinking.

MATERIALS

1. Keep materials simple and to a minimum. It takes more problem solving to adapt and manage with less rather than to simply buy more.

2. Avoid problem-solving tasks that waste food. Many people consider food waste an inappropriate model in our classrooms when up to 20 percent of our nation's children live in poverty (Payne, 1995).

3. Involve students in collecting and preparing most of the free or recycled materials required in these problems. This procedure increases students' responsibility and decreases teacher preparation time.

4. Accent tasks that minimize the cost of materials. Brainstorm alternatives to materials that are costly or difficult to acquire.

ATTITUDE

1. Trust your students to expand their creative thinking as they gain more experience going beyond simple right answers. At first, some students are reluctant to create new ideas as they are accustomed to second guessing answers others have in mind.

2. Avoid a one-way attitude. Creative problem solving should encourage many different approaches and solutions. Expect to see and hear group ideas that vary substantially from what you anticipated.

Kingore, B. (1998). Engaging Creative Thinking. Austin: Professional Associates Publishing

3. Encourage students to risk divergent ideas rather than limit themselves to the expected.

4. Marilyn Vos Savant (1997) offers an anecdote to share with students who do not consider themselves creative. Before limiting themselves in what they think they can do, ask students to consider the bumblebee. The bumblebee is an aerodynamically-unsound, little creature whose body is far too large, his wings are far too small, and he has hair instead of feathers. Judging his qualifications on paper, we would have to say that he could not possibly fly. But the bumblebee does not know this, so he flies merrily away! Engage students in problem solving performance tasks and let them fly to new heights with productive ideas and solutions.

REFLECTIONS FOR TEACHERS:
INCREASING THE VALUE OF PERFORMANCE TASKS

Metacognition is vital for teachers who intend to maximize the educational value of students' problem solving. Enhance future learning by reviewing students' performance, analyzing their process and progress, and identifying desired changes. Consider the following questions as prompts to your reflection.

1. **Process and Criteria**
    *   How does each criterion add to the problem solving required in the task?
    *   Why are specific items required?
    *   What is the purpose of the time limit?
    *   What would change if this task was completed in a large group or by individuals?
    *   How might you insure that all students are actively involved in as equal a manner as possible?

2. **Effectiveness and Appropriateness**
    *   Are the criteria developmentally appropriate for the age and background of your students?
    *   Does the project allow for differentiation of students' readiness levels?
    *   Which part causes students the greatest difficulty? Why? Should that part be altered, or is it an appropriate challenge?

3. **Group Dynamics**
    *   Who started the task? How?
    *   Some groups jump right into the task while others stop to plan and organize first. Was one approach more successful or efficient?
    *   Which students stayed on task? Who did not? Why or why not?

Kingore, B. (1998). Engaging Creative Thinking. Austin: Professional Associates Publishing

- Analyze each student's role as several different roles typically emerge.
  a. Director/learner: "You could _____ while he _____."
  b. Mathematician: "We need three more. See here we have one-two-three-four..." "If we increase the angle here..."
  c. Problem solver: "We could change..."
  d. Materials gatherer: "We need to get a ..."
  e. Design specialist "Oh, this would look nice." "It would be stronger if..."
  f. Encourager: "I like your..."

4. Thinking Skills
- Which high-level thinking skills were demonstrated?
- Were most of the questions students ask each other during this task: "Why," "How could we," "What about," or "What if" prompts?
- What positive comments did you make to students regarding their thinking?

5. AFFECTIVE DOMAIN
- How did this project allow for affective needs?
- What affective issues surfaced during this project?

6. Increasing the Value of a Task
- How could you make this project more effective next time?
- How do you plan to vary this task to increase content value?
- How can you adapt this construction problem to more effectively incorporate other concepts and skills?
- How should the activity be altered to solve any problems?
- What changes do students suggest for future use?

7. Instructional Effectiveness
- What important attributes have you learned about your students during this construction problem?
- What questions did you pose as you observed your students work?
- How effective were you as a facilitator during this simulation? Did you station yourself in one area of the classroom or observe from various locations?

- How did you reach the diversity of intelligences and learning styles represented in your class?
- What gifted behaviors were demonstrated during these tasks? Be alert to advanced language, complex analytical thinking, an intense drive for meaning, perspective, high-level humor, sensitivity, and advanced levels of content (Kingore, 2001). For example, did you hear a child use advanced language to explain an idea to another child in a sequential

manner? Did a student use similes or metaphors to express relation-ships? Keep an anecdotal record or KOI tally of your observations for future information during parent conferences, gifted nominations, or other assessments (Kingore, 2001).

- Select two students you observed whose behaviors or thinking skills deserve acknowledgment and reinforcement. Call their parent(s) to share your observations and celebrate the child's success with them! It takes five minutes out of your day, but consider what this strategy may communicate to parents and students about your priorities.

- Observe your teaching style. Video-tape yourself facilitating these tasks. When watching the tape, analyze if you interact more with one gender than the other. Do you provide equal time with all students? Do you comment more on the value of students' thinking or the aesthetic significance of their work? Think about it.

DEVELOPING NEW CREATIVE PROBLEM-SOLVING TASKS

Applying the format in this book, develop your own creative problem solving tasks relating to any unit of study. The following list is intended to suggest possible tasks to incorporate.

Build a house for each of the three little pigs.
- Use a hair dryer or fan to test the strength of each house.

Create a floating device that can carry a certain amount of cargo across a pan of water.
- Use fishing weights, coins, or marbles for the weight.
- Have the students blow on it or use a fan for wind power to move it across the water.

Create supply holders to organize classroom and centers' equipment.
- Cover cans to hold pencils and markers.
- Create storage boxes made from folded paper.
- Create trays from cardboard boxes for organizing large items.

Create a habitat for an endangered species or a classroom pet.
- Make a habitat for a hermit crab.
- Make a hiding place for a hamster.

Alphabet Constructions
- Read Albert's Alphabet by Leslie Tryon. Let children create each letter from a different material.
- Use play dough in different colors for vowels and consonants and codify the pattern.

Kingore, B. (1998). Engaging Creative Thinking. Austin: Professional Associates Publishing

NOTES

Architecture
- Create multiple-sided, three-dimensional units to represent geometric structures in nature, e.g., bee hives and geodesic dome structures.

Airplanes
- Use paper of different sizes and weights. Create airplanes that meet different criteria, e.g., travel the farthest, remain in air the longest, and turn in flight.

FORMAT FOR DEVELOPING NEW CREATIVE PROBLEM SOLVING TASKS

TITLE: _____

_____

GRADE LEVEL(S): _____

_____

CONTENT AREAS: _____

_____

PROBLEM: _____

_____

MATERIALS: _____

_____

BACKGROUND: _____

_____

CRITERIA: _____

_____

PROCEDURE: _____

_____

EVALUATION: _____

_____

EXTENSIONS FOR STUDENTS: _____

_____

REFLECTION FOR TEACHERS: _____

_____

SPECIAL NOTES: _____

_____

STUDENT COPY AND HANDOUTS: _____

_____

Kingore, B. (1998). Engaging Creative Thinking. Austin: Professional Associates Publishing

THE ALIEN

Bertie Kingore, Bonnie Hood, and Julia Griffin

GRADE LEVELS
Kindergarten through sixth grade

CONTENT CONNECTION
Art, language arts, math, science, and social studies

PROBLEM
Students work in groups primarily using recyclable materials to build a three-dimensional alien that is exactly two feet tall and free standing.

MATERIALS

1. Masking tape--one roll for each team

2. Scissors--one pair for each student

3. Recyclable trash for building materials--each team is limited to 15 items, e.g., aluminum cans, boxes, plastic containers, and newspapers

4. One 12-inch ruler for each team

BACKGROUND

1. MEASUREMENT CONCEPTS.
   a. Standard units of measurement
   b. Different rulers and their uses
   c. The metric system

NOTES

Kingore, B. (1998). <u>Engaging Creative Thinking</u>. Austin: Professional Associates Publishing

NOTES

2. ESTIMATION.
   a. Discuss estimation techniques.
   b. Model the Estimation Checklist on page 28 to record data.

3. Review cooperative learning and team building.

4. Demonstrate different graphs and how to read them.

5. Discuss the three R's--reduce, recycle, and reuse. With the students' help, list items typically thrown away in daily use can be recycled or reused.

CRITERIA

1. Each team's alien must be exactly two feet tall. Notice how they figure out how to complete that measurement using only one 12-inch-ruler.

2. It must be made from exactly 15 recyclable or reusable items. Each item is defined by its original state, e.g., a cardboard roll cut in half is still counted as one item.
   Note: For safety with younger students, exclude glass and other objects with sharp edges.

3. It must be free standing.

4. It must be sturdy enough to be moved without breaking.

5. Each construction team has 50 minutes to design and assemble an alien.

PROCEDURE

FIRST DAY

1. COOPERATIVE GROUPS. Groups of three or four are preferable to encourage diverse ideas while increasing active participation.

2. TEAM PLANNING. Students brainstorm as a team.
   a. What will the alien look like, and how will that reflect its abilities?
   b. What kinds of recyclable or reusable items are needed to make it two feet tall?
   c. How can it be constructed so that it stands by itself?
   d. What recyclable items from home should each person try to collect? (More than fifteen items should be collected.)

SECOND DAY

1. Students bring recyclable materials to school.

Kingore, B. (1998). Engaging Creative Thinking. Austin: Professional Associates Publishing

2. Each team selects 15 items from the materials collected by that group. All members of the team assemble the alien and then clean their work area.

   Note: This section of the task may be divided into two sessions of 25 minutes each if one 50-minute session is not appropriate for your students or conducive to your schedule.

3. BIOGRAPHY. Have students write a biography of their alien, including the following information.
   a. What is your alien's name? Does that have a meaning?
   b. What should we know about its family?
   c. Where is your alien from? How does that place resemble or differ from Earth?
   d. How did it get here? Draw a diagram of its vehicle.
   e. What are its nutritional needs? Can it survive on food available in the cafeteria?
   f. Describe six characteristics of your alien.
   g. What special powers or abilities does your alien have that help people? How are these reflected in the alien's construction?
   h. Why is it at your school?
   i. Create an immigration card registering the alien with school authorities so it is not an illegal visitor.

4. AWARDS. Children create an award for their alien based on its characteristics such as friendliest, most unique, funniest, or best use of materials. Nurture self-esteem by ensuring that there is an equally desirable award available for every creation and that every alien receives an award.

THIRD DAY

1. ESTIMATION. Using observation and analysis, each team observes the finished aliens of the other groups and then estimates which aliens are exactly two feet tall. On the provided Estimation Checklist, one member records the team's estimate of the height of each alien. Challenge the students to specify in one-quarter-inch increments if the alien is more or less than two feet.
   a. To control the noise level, require the students to use personal-level voices that can only be heard within a few inches as they analyze and estimate.
   b. Accent that the teams may not touch or measure the aliens. All estimations must be based on observation.

2. MEASUREMENT. The teacher, or other designated adult, measures each alien as the children watch. Teams record the data in the last column on their Estimation Checklist.

Kingore, B. (1998). <u>Engaging Creative Thinking</u>. Austin: Professional Associates Publishing

NOTES

3. BAR GRAPH. The class completes a bar graph comparing the heights of all the aliens. Older students graph the heights as percentages of two feet by dividing the actual height by two.

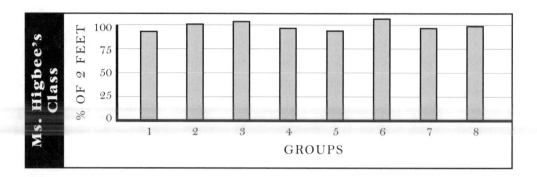

4. GREATER THAN OR LESS THAN. Discuss which aliens are greater than or less than two feet tall. Using increments of one quarter inch, measure the differences, and discuss what might be done to alter the alien to meet specifications. To extend learning, older students convert differences in heights to ratios or percentages.

5. Display the aliens for all to compare, contrast, photograph, and enjoy.

6. EVALUATION. Each team collaborates to complete an Evaluation. It is intended as a metacognitive response for group awareness but may be used as a recorded grade. When used as a recorded grade, the team completes their evaluation first. The teacher then evaluates the team on the same sheet. Discussing any differences with the students enhances the learning potential of the evaluation process.

LATER

When interest in the completed aliens wanes, each group takes apart their alien and sorts the items according to their recyclable category. Arrange for the items to be delivered to a recycling center.

EXTENSIONS FOR STUDENTS

1. DISCUSSION. Discuss the concepts of reducing, recycling, and reusing.
   a. Which categories of materials are not recyclable or reusable? Why?
   b. Discuss the similarities and differences between recyclable and non-recyclable materials.
   c. Discuss scarcity and environmental impact.

Kingore, B. (1998). Engaging Creative Thinking. Austin: Professional Associates Publishing

    d. Using a map of the community, plot the location of recycling centers. If recycling centers are not available, research who has the power to establish them. What might the class do to influence this change?

2. METRIC MEASUREMENT. Remeasure the alien using metric tools to demonstrate the metric system, and compare it to standard measurement.

3. INSTRUCTIONAL SHAPE BOOK. Each child draws and cuts out blank pages in an alien shape to staple together, and create an alien shape book.
    a. Each child writes and illustrates a story about the alien and its adventures in the community.
    b. Each child writes an informational booklet about how to construct aliens using recyclable materials, including a parts list and warranty.

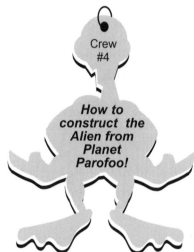

4. EXPOSITORY WRITING. As a variation of the shape book, incorporate sequencing and following-directions skills by having each group write the step-by-step procedure to duplicate their alien construction. Others, without looking at the original, read the directions and try to assemble a matching alien twin. When completed, the groups compare the original alien and its twin. Use a Venn diagram to record the results and post a photograph of each construction on the appropriate side of the Venn.

5. VIDEO. Tape portions of the construction procedure for the students to view later. Ensure that all of the children appear on the video, and include each finished product.
    a. Show the tape at a parent night or during Education Week.
    b. When viewing the tape, give examples of the types of questions students asked during the construction process. Point out the examples of high-level thinking that are demonstrated.
    c. Allow the video to be checked out for sharing with families at home.

6. TOPIC VARIATIONS. The problem may be adapted to implement with different units. The following are examples of possible topic connections.
    a. Nutrition: Balanced Foods Friend
    b. Ecology: Save the Earth Creature, or Pollution Elimination Machine
    c. Tools and Machines: Machine with a Special Function
    d. Fantasy: Monster

Kingore, B. (1998). <u>Engaging Creative Thinking</u>. Austin: Professional Associates Publishing

THE ALIEN: STUDENT COPY
Bertie Kingore, Bonnie Hood, and Julia Griffin

PROBLEM

Work in groups primarily using recyclable materials to build a three-dimensional alien that is exactly two feet tall and free standing.

MATERIALS

1. Masking tape--one roll for each team

2. Scissors--one pair for each child

3. Recyclable trash for building materials--each team is limited to 15 items, e.g., aluminum cans, boxes, cardboard, plastic containers, cardboard rolls, and newspapers

4. One 12-inch ruler for each team

CRITERIA

1. Your team's alien must be exactly two feet tall. How can you accurately measure it using only one 12-inch-ruler?

2. It must be made from exactly 15 recyclable or reusable items.

3. It must be free standing.

4. It must be sturdy enough to be moved without breaking.

5. Each construction team will have 50 minutes to design and assemble it.

PROCEDURE

FIRST DAY

Brainstorm as a team:
a. What will your alien look like, and how will that reflect its abilities?
b. What kinds of recyclable or reusable items are needed to make it two feet tall?
c. How can you construct it so that it stands by itself?
d. What recyclable items from home should each person try to bring to class? (More than 15 items should be collected.)

Kingore, B. (1998). <u>Engaging Creative Thinking</u>. Austin: Professional Associates Publishing

SECOND DAY

1. Bring recyclable materials to school.

2. Select 15 items from the collected materials. Work as a team to construct the alien and then clean the work area.

3. BIOGRAPHY. Together, write a biography of your alien including the following information.
   a. What is your alien's name? Does it have a meaning?
   b. What should we know about its family?
   c. Where is your alien from? How does that place resemble or differ from Earth?
   d. How did it get here? Draw a diagram of its vehicle.
   e. What are its nutritional needs? Can it survive on food available in the cafeteria?
   f. Describe six characteristics of your alien.
   g. What special powers or abilities does your alien have that help people?
   h. Why is it at your school?
   i. Create an immigration card registering the alien with school authorities so it is not an illegal visitor.

4. AWARDS. Create an award for your alien based on its characteristics, e.g., the friendliest, most unique, funniest, or best use of materials.

5. In an oral presentation, share your alien, biography, and award to the class.

THIRD DAY

1. ESTIMATION. Work together to observe the completed aliens of the other groups. Estimate which aliens are exactly two feet tall. On the Estimation Checklist, one member records the team's estimate of each alien's height. Specify in one-quarter-inch increments if the alien is greater than or less than two feet.
   a. Use personal-level voices that can only be heard within a few inches as you discuss your estimations.
   b. Do not touch or measure the aliens. All estimations are based on observation.

2. MEASUREMENT. The teacher, or other designated adult, measures each alien as the teams watch. Record the data in the last column on the Estimation Checklist.

3. BAR GRAPH. As a class, complete a bar graph comparing the heights of all the aliens, and discuss which aliens are greater than or less than two feet tall. How could the aliens be adjusted to meet the specifications?

4. EVALUATION. Each team collaborates to complete an Evaluation.

Kingore, B. (1998). <u>Engaging Creative Thinking</u>. Austin: Professional Associates Publishing

THE ALIEN
ESTIMATION CHECKLIST

GROUP _____   DATE _____

	Is the alien exactly two feet tall? 👍	👎	ESTIMATE + MORE	− LESS	MEASURED HEIGHT
GROUPS	YES	NO	MORE	LESS	
1.					
2.					
3.					
4.					
5.					
6.					
7.					
8.					
9.					
10.					
11.					
12.					

Kingore, B. (1998). <u>Engaging Creative Thinking</u>. Austin: Professional Associates Publishing

THE ALIEN
EVALUATION

NAMES _____

DATE _____

Construction: 50 total points

___ / 10   1. Our alien's measured height is _____.

___ / 10   2. Exactly 15 recyclable or reusable items are used.

___ / 10   3. The alien is free standing.

___ / 10   4. The alien is sturdy enough to be moved without breaking.

___ / 10   5. Our team finished on time.

Cooperation: ___ / 30 points

To work well together, our team _____

_____

_____.

One idea to help our team work even better is _____

_____

_____.

Estimation: ___ / 20 points

To complete our estimation, we _____

_____.

Our estimations might be even better if _____

_____.

Suggestion

Something we could have done differently is _____

_____.

Kingore, B. (1998). Engaging Creative Thinking. Austin: Professional Associates Publishing

THE ALIEN: CONCEPTS AND SKILLS

ART
Exploring art elements of line, shape, texture, form, and space
Expressing ideas in three-dimensional form

LANGUAGE ARTS
Classifying by similarities and/or differences
Listening to instructions and listening to others
Oral communication
Reading and following directions
Writing for a variety of purposes

MATH
Constructing and interpreting bar graphs
Estimation
Measurement and measurement tools
Number concepts
Recognizing simple and compound fractions

SCIENCE
Balance (physics)
Classifying objects from the environment
Ecology
Anatomy (biology)

SOCIAL STUDIES
Accepting responsibility
Compromising and building consensus
Cooperative learning
Group interaction
Responsibility
Standards of honesty and fairness
Task commitment

THINKING SKILLS
Analytical thinking
Comparing and contrasting
Evaluation
Planning
Organizing
Synthesizing

OTHERS
_____
_____
_____
_____
_____

Kingore, B. (1998). Engaging Creative Thinking. Austin: Professional Associates Publishing

NEWSPAPER BRIDGES

Kim Cheek

GRADE LEVELS
First through eighth grade

CONTENT CONNECTION
Language arts, math, science, and social studies

PROBLEM
Students use newspaper and tape to build a standing bridge that is a minimum of 6 inches tall, 12 inches long, and supports a minimum of 4 pounds for 60 seconds.

MATERIALS

1. Newspapers--a two-inch stack for each group

2. Masking tape--one roll for each group

3. Ruler--one per group

4. Construction paper-one sheet per group for the name and dedication sign of the bridge

5. Large trash bags for clean-up

6. A stop watch or watch with a second hand to use during strength testing

7. OPTIONAL: A digital or traditional camera with film for recording the work of the construction companies or a camcorder for videotaping the process

NOTES

Kingore, B. (1998). <u>Engaging Creative Thinking</u>. Austin: Professional Associates Publishing

NOTES | **BACKGROUND**

1. MEASUREMENT
   a. Discuss bridge sizes.
      • The longest bridge in the world crosses Lake Pontchartrain in Louisiana. This bridge has two causeways that measure 48 miles.
      • The Humber Estuary Bridge in northern England was opened in 1981. It is a suspension bridge with a length of 7,280 feet.
   b. Discuss the standard and metric system as units of measurement.
   c. Compare the ruler, yardstick, and meter stick. What other tools might a crew use to measure their structures?

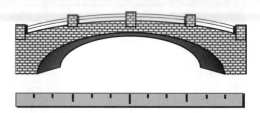

2. Discuss the reasons construction crews must cooperate when building bridges.

3. Discuss the three R's--reduce, recycle, and reuse. How might this Earth-friendly strategy effect the new bridges of the 21st century?

4. Bridges
   a. Discuss the concept of bridges.
      • Bridges allow us to cross natural or man-made obstructions.
      • Not all bridges are man-made.
   b. Discuss types of bridges including arch, suspension, and cantilever.
   c. Challenge students to bring pictures of bridges to categorize and label the different structural elements.
      • The deck is the part that carries the path, road, or railroad.
      • The abutments are the supports at each end of the bridge.
      • The piers are the vertical or upright supports.
      • The span is the section of a bridge that lies between two piers.
      • The main span is the longest.
   d. Assign individuals or small groups one of the following to investigate and present to the class: bridges that move, how suspension bridges are built, a natural bridge, the oldest bridge (the Clapper bridges of southwest England), an aqueduct (a bridge that is designed to carry water), the widest bridge (The Sydney Harbor Bridge in Australia--160 feet across), the highest bridge (The Royal Gorge of the Arkansas River in Colorado--1,053 feet high).

COUNTY CONSTRUCTION REGULATIONS

1. The bridge must be a minimum of 6 inches tall.

2. It must be a minimum of 12 inches long.

Kingore, B. (1998). Engaging Creative Thinking. Austin: Professional Associates Publishing

3. It must be free standing.

4. It must be sturdy enough to hold and support a minimum of 4 pounds for 60 seconds.

5. Only newspaper and tape can be used to construct the bridge.

6. Each construction crew has _____ minutes to construct their bridge.

7. Each crew creates a dedication plaque for their bridge. It should honor a person, place, or concept studied this year.

PROCEDURE

Ask students to bring newspapers from home. If the papers are rolled, unroll and stack them flat until ready for construction. Collect for a couple of weeks, depending upon the number of students participating.

SEQUENCE OF BRIDGE CONSTRUCTIONS

1. Assign students in groups to form construction crews. Crews of three or four encourage diverse ideas and active participation.

2. Each crew brainstorms a company name to use during construction and posts that name at their site.

3. Each company establishes its credentials as bridge experts by brainstorming for five minutes as many bridge connections as they can list on paper. Encourage students to think of bridges in books, songs, and games, e.g., the card game of bridge, the song: "Bridge Over Troubled Water", the book <u>Bridge to Teribithia</u>, and dental bridgework. You may have a team make more abstract connections with analogies such as: "Education is a bridge to the future," and "Books are a bridge to adventures."

4. OPTIONAL: Each company develops a collage displaying their brainstormed credentials.

5. Construction crews design and construct a newspaper bridge meeting all county regulations. The County Inspector, a.k.a., the teacher or principal, establishes the maximum building time most appropriate for the age group. Younger students may need 60 to 90 minutes while older groups may complete the problem in 45 minutes. The total construction time may be divided into smaller segments over several days rather than completed in one day.

Kingore, B. (1998). <u>Engaging Creative Thinking</u>. Austin: Professional Associates Publishing

NOTES

STRENGTH REINFORCEMENT EXPERIMENTS. Manipulating newspaper in different ways affects its strength. Students experiment by folding, layering, twisting, rolling, and wadding the layers of paper. They test each method for strength and record the results.

BLUEPRINTS. Each company sketches their design plan and submits their final blueprint to the County Inspector for approval. The County Inspector documents that each bridge design meets county regulations.

CLASSROOM MANAGEMENT. County regulations have strict noise pollution and environmental guidelines:
1. Crews must use personal-level voices and work as a team.
2. The county will not replace misused materials. Care and budgeting of a crew's resources must be exercised.
3. Crews may not touch another company's bridge.

PROCEDURE AFTER CONSTRUCTIONS ARE COMPLETED

1. Crews clean their work areas.

2. Crews brainstorm ideas for naming their bridge, designing a plaque for the dedication, and presenting their bridge to the class.

3. The County Inspector measures each bridge to assure compliance with county regulations.

4. The County Inspector monitors the strength test of each bridge. Each bridge must support a minimum of 4 pounds for 60 seconds. Each crew determines placement of the weight on their bridge for the test. The County Inspector uses a watch to time the test.

   HELPFUL HINT: Have a student weigh individual encyclopedias and record the weight. Use those books to document bridge strength.

5. EVALUATION. Each team collaborates to complete the Evaluation or Rubric. Utilize the form most appropriate for your students' ages and abilities.

CLEAN-UP

After the bridges are photographed, admired, and tested, place the materials into trash bags for delivery to a recycling container or center. As a class, discuss the impact of recycling. In what other ways can the students recycle? What are ways in which the school might increase recycling efforts?

Kingore, B. (1998). Engaging Creative Thinking. Austin: Professional Associates Publishing

EXTENSIONS FOR STUDENTS

1. NEWSPAPER ARTICLE. Individually or as a team, students write an article reporting the bridge dedication ceremony.

2. Younger students read different versions of <u>The Three Billy Goat's Gruff</u> and compare the styles of bridge illustrations in each. Allow students to use puppets and the bridge they constructed to act out the story.

3. STATISTICS FOR CLASS CONSTRUCTION LOG.
   a. Which team built the strongest bridge? Teams who want to participate in this category continue to add weight until the bridge collapses. Calculate the amount the bridge successfully held.
   b. Which team built the longest bridge? Measure for length.
   c. Which team built the tallest bridge? Measure for height.
   d. Which bridge incorporated an original design?

4. METRIC MEASUREMENT. Have students remeasure using metric measurements.

5. DEVELOP ANALOGIES. "Bridges are like _____ because _____" "I am like a bridge when _____"

6. Take pictures of students during the task. Photos duplicate easily on a copy machine. Place a photo on a blank piece of paper with room for students to write about the activity and the challenge it provided.

7. RESEARCH. Have students research famous bridges throughout the world. Using a world map, students document the location on a Post-it Note™ and place it on the map. Challenge crews to develop a travel brochure sharing information and illustrations.

8. Discuss people in history, current events, and characters in fiction who serve as a bridge in some way, e.g., Mother Theresa was a bridge to unconditional human compassion.

9. Research construction regulations for your city or county. Who is responsible? Where are the regulations recorded? What procedures are required to get a building permit? Are different offices or government agencies involved if the bridge is a city, county, or national structure?

10. TOPIC VARIATIONS. Vary the task to implement construction problems with different units. For example, during a rain forest unit, students construct an environmentally friendly observation tower or bridge for scientists.

Kingore, B. (1998). <u>Engaging Creative Thinking</u>. Austin: Professional Associates Publishing

NEWSPAPER BRIDGES: STUDENT COPY
Kim Cheek

PROBLEM

Work in groups using newspaper and tape to build a standing bridge that is a minimum of 6 inches tall, is 12 inches long, and supports a minimum of 4 pounds for 60 seconds.

MATERIALS

1. Newspapers - a stack one or two inches tall for each group

2. Masking tape - one roll for each group

3. Ruler - one per group

4. Construction paper - one sheet per group for name and dedication sign of bridge

5. Large trash bags for clean-up

6. A stop watch or watch with a second hand to use during strength testing

   OPTIONAL: A camera to record the work of the construction companies or a camcorder to videotape the process

COUNTY CONSTRUCTION REGULATIONS

1. The bridge must be a minimum of 6 inches tall.

2. It must be a minimum of 12 inches long.

3. It must be free standing.

4. It must be sturdy enough to support a minimum of 4 pounds for 60 seconds.

5. Use only newspaper and tape to construct the bridge.

6. Your construction crew has _____ minutes to construct your bridge.

7. Create a dedication plaque for your bridge. It should honor a person, place, or concept studied this year.

Kingore, B. (1998). <u>Engaging Creative Thinking</u>. Austin: Professional Associates Publishing

SEQUENCE OF BRIDGE CONSTRUCTION

1. Form a construction crew of three or four people.
   a. Brainstorm a construction company name to use while building. Post the name at your construction site.
   b. Establish your credentials as bridge experts by brainstorming for five minutes as many connections to bridges as you can list on paper. Think of bridges in books, songs, history, or games.

2. Design and construct a newspaper bridge that meets all county regulations. Your crew has _____ minutes to plan and construct your bridge.

STRENGTH REINFORCEMENT EXPERIMENTS. Manipulate newspaper in different ways to affect its strength. Experiment by folding, layering, twisting, rolling, and wadding the layers of paper. Test each method for strength and record the results.

BLUEPRINTS. Sketch design plans; submit your final blueprint to the County Inspector, a.k.a., the teacher, for approval. The County Inspector documents that the bridge meets county regulations.

> NOISE POLLUTION AND ENVIRONMENTAL GUIDELINES:
> 1. Crews must use personal-level voices and work as a team.
> 2. The county will not replace misused materials. Care and budgeting of a crew's resources must be exercised.
> 3. Crews may not touch another company's bridge.

PROCEDURE AFTER CONSTRUCTIONS ARE COMPLETED

1. CLEAN UP. Crews clean their work area.

2. DEDICATION. Brainstorm ideas for naming your bridge. After reaching consensus, design a plaque for the dedication ceremony, and present your bridge to the class.

3. MEASUREMENT. The County Inspector measures each bridge to assure compliance with county regulations.

4. STRENGTH TEST. The County Inspector monitors the strength test of each bridge. Each bridge must support a minimum of 4 pounds for 60 seconds. Your crew determines the placement of the weight on the bridge, and the County Inspector uses a stop watch to time the test.

5. EVALUATION. Team members collaborate to complete the Evaluation or Rubric.

Kingore, B. (1998). <u>Engaging Creative Thinking</u>. Austin: Professional Associates Publishing

NEWSPAPER BRIDGES
EVALUATION

NAMES _____

DATE _____

Construction: 70 total points

___ / 10   Only newspaper and tape are used in the construction.

___ / 10   The bridge was completed on time.

___ / 10   The bridge is free standing.

___ / 10   The bridge is a minimum of 6 inches high.

___ / 10   The bridge is a minimum of 12 inches long.

___ / 10   The bridge supports a minimum of 4 pounds for 60 seconds.

___ / 10   The bridge is named according to the criteria.

Cooperation: ___ / 30 points

To help us work well together, our team _____

_____

_____.

One idea to help our group work even better would be _____

_____.

One thing our crew enjoyed most about this activity was _____

_____

_____.

Our crew used the following thinking skills:

• _____   • _____

• _____   • _____

Our special message to the teacher is _____

_____.

Kingore, B. (1998). Engaging Creative Thinking. Austin: Professional Associates Publishing

NEWSPAPER BRIDGES
RUBRIC

NAME _____   DATE _____

CRITERIA	NOVICE	APPRENTICE	PROFICIENT ASSISTANT	ADVANCED ENGINEER
Building Plan Points _____/20	Did not complete a blueprint 1-2	Completed a blueprint but did not build to plan 3-8	Built to plan with limited assistance 9-14	Built to plan; no prompting; self-motivated 15-20
Creativity Points _____/20	Used others' ideas or responses 1-2	Typical response; little original thinking 3-8	Creative integration; enhanced responses 9-14	Unique ideas; insightful; novel 15-20
Integration of Skills Points _____/20	Unable to apply skills 1-2	Attempted to integrate skills and information 3-8	Accurate integration of skills 9-14	Effective in process and product 15-20
Problem Solving Points _____/20	Inappropriate process 1-2	Incomplete or limited application; logic is flawed 3-8	Appropriate process; analysis and application are evident 9-14	High-level solution; innovative; synthesized; evaluated 15-20
Group Cooperation Points _____/10	Inappropriate; resistant 1	Appropriate cooperation 2-4	Listened attentively; helped others; shared 5-7	Encouraged and redirected others back to task; negotiated 8-10
Effort/Task Commitment Points _____/10	Resistant 1	Inadequate for task; incomplete 2-4	Appropriate effort; successful 5-7	Extensive effort; used time well 8-10

Kingore, B. (1998). Engaging Creative Thinking. Austin: Professional Associates Publishing

NEWSPAPER BRIDGES: CONCEPTS AND SKILLS

LANGUAGE ARTS

Using analogies
Classifying by similarities and/or differences
Listening to instructions and to others
Oral communication
Oral presentation
Reading and following directions
Writing for a variety of purposes

MATH

Categorizing
Construction
Estimation
Measurement: Standard and Metric systems
Problem solving

SCIENCE

Balance
Ecology
Experimental research
Factual observation
Interpreting data

SOCIAL STUDIES

Compromising and building consensus
Expressing emotions appropriately
Goal setting
Group cooperation and group dynamics
Leadership
Respecting and accepting diverse ideas
Accepting responsibility
Risk taking
Task commitment and time management

THINKING SKILLS

Analytical thinking
Brainstorming - fluency & flexibility
Elaboration
Evaluation
Problem identification
Synthesizing

OTHERS

_____
_____
_____

Kingore, B. (1998). Engaging Creative Thinking. Austin: Professional Associates Publishing

ARCHITECTURE

Mary Christopher

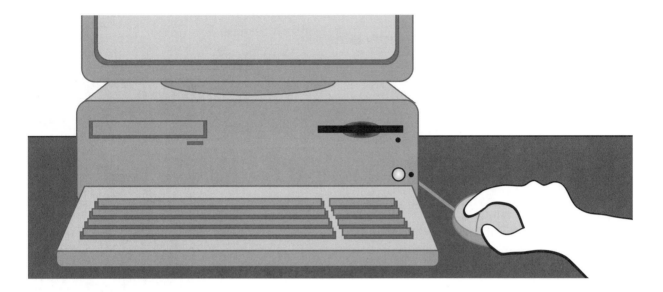

GRADE LEVELS

Second through twelfth grade

CONTENT CONNECTION

Art, language arts, math, science, social studies, and technology applications

ESSENTIAL QUESTIONS

1. What types of geometric patterns and shapes are used in the architecture of industrial, commercial, and residential buildings?

2. How are these types of structures similar and different?

PROBLEM

Using the drawing feature of an integrated computer software package, students replicate the facade of one commercial or industrial building and one residential building. Students compare the geometric features and patterns found in the architectural structure of each building.

MATERIALS

1. Building materials, e.g., wooden blocks of various shapes, straws, tongue depressors, Duplos™, Legos™, and Lincoln Logs™

Kingore, B. (1998). Engaging Creative Thinking. Austin: Professional Associates Publishing

NOTES

2. Integrated computer software package

3. Computer Aided Design (CAD) software

4. Camera (digital camera preferred)

5. Printer

BACKGROUND

1. MATHEMATICAL CONCEPTS.
    a. Geometric figures
    b. Patterns
    c. Symmetry/asymmetry

2. COMPUTER SCIENCE.
    a. Graphic design
    b. Application of drawing software

3. FINE ARTS.
    a. Design
    b. Art history
        i. Periods of architecture, e.g., Colonial, Federal, Victorian, Elizabethan, Gothic, Art Deco, Art Nouveau
        ii. Cultural styles of architecture, e.g., adobe huts, pyramids, castles, skyscrapers
    c. Architectural elements
        Provide a copy of the glossary on the next page. Help your students learn to identify different architectural elements.
    d. Architects--four examples follow

Alexandre Gustave Eiffel (1832-1923)
A French engineer and entrepreneur, he designed many bridges as well as the Eiffel Tower.

Thomas Jefferson (1743-1826)
He adapted ancient Roman architecture to design the Virginia State Capitol which became the model for public buildings in America.

Leonardo da Vinci (1452-1519)
A genius, artist, and scientist of the Italian Renaissance, he left behind numerous building plans and designs.

Frank Lloyd Wright (1869-1959)
His contemporary Prairie style was influenced by the nature around each building. His designs influenced many later developments in architecture.

Kingore, B. (1998). Engaging Creative Thinking. Austin: Professional Associates Publishing

GLOSSARY OF ARCHITECTURE

ARCADE. The arrangement of several arches in a row is called an arcade

ARCH. Vaulted structure in a wall opening or hall

ATRIUM. Central courtyard in the roman residential building

BALUSTRADE. A parapet (railing) consisting of rows of small columns (balusters)

BLIND ARCADE, BLIND ARCH, BLIND WINDOW. The elements of one applied to a wall without any architectural purpose

BUTTRESSING, FLYING BUTTRESS, PIER BUTTRESS. Skeleton structure used in the reinforcement of high walls

CANTILEVER. A level projecting from a building that is not supported from beneath

CLERESTORY (WINDOWS). Upper area of the walls of the nave with windows

COLUMN. Circularly-shaped, vertical beam, usually supporting the roof

COLONNADE. Rows of columns with vertical entablature.

CORINTHIAN. Classical Greek style; ornate columns

DOME. A hemisphere-shaped roof

DORIC. The oldest Classic Greek style; plain design and no flutes on columns

FACADE. The exterior face of a building

FLUTES. Vertical ridges along the shaft of ancient columns

IONIC. The second oldest Classic Greek style

KEYSTONE. Central stone of an arch or rib vault

NAVE. In churches, the elongated section of the building

PILASTER. Vertical pillar with a base and capital projecting from a wall

PILLAR. A free-standing, rectangularly-shaped variation of a column

PORTICO. An open space covered by a roof supported on columns or pillars

POST AND LINTEL. A building construction of a post supporting each end of a beam

PYRAMID. Ancient tomb or shrine most associated with Egyptians but found across the world; structure of four walls meeting at one point

RIBS. The load-bearing structures of a ceiling

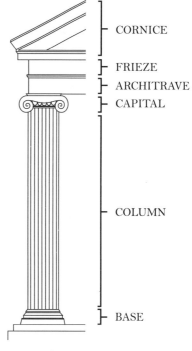

COLUMN--IONIC

Kingore, B. (1998). Engaging Creative Thinking. Austin: Professional Associates Publishing

NOTES

CRITERIA

This is a open-ended assignment with criteria dependent on the age-level and readiness of the student. The teacher adjusts the criteria to meet the expectations for the class.

1. The completed drawings should be clear replicas of the chosen buildings.

2. The analysis and comparison of two types of buildings should show a clear understanding of geometric shapes, patterns, symmetry, architectural features, and/or periods of architecture.

3. The product of this project should include the original pictures, computer-drawn replicas of one commercial or industrial building and one residential building, and a written analysis comparing the two buildings. The product format is student selected.

PROCEDURE

1. Place transparencies of building facades on the overhead projector. Let students identify geometric shapes and architectural elements found in the buildings by outlining those shapes on the transparencies. Discuss the use of geometry and pattern in the design of buildings.

2. Review different periods of architecture. Then, guide students to identify several different characteristics that represent specific periods and cultural styles of the structures.

3. Identify examples of symmetry and asymmetry in the buildings. Discuss how architects use symmetry and asymmetry to make buildings aesthetically pleasing or unique. Explain architecture as a form of fine art.

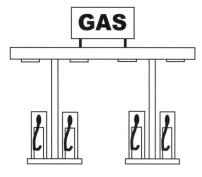

PRIMARY STUDENT EXAMPLE:
A GAS STATION

4. Using a digital camera, tour a commercial or industrial area close to the school. Photograph a variety of different buildings to use as class examples. Upon returning to school, download these pictures into the computer and print them out. If a digital camera is not available, use a regular camera and have the pictures developed for the next day.

Kingore, B. (1998). Engaging Creative Thinking. Austin: Professional Associates Publishing

5. Ask students to bring pictures of residences, either photographs or cuttings from magazines. Some students may bring pictures of their own residences to analyze the architecture.

6. Allow students to choose building materials to make a three-dimensional model of their buildings. More advanced students may not need this concrete approach, but it will help many students develop a geometric understanding of the structures.

SECONDARY STUDENT EXAMPLE:
A FARM HOUSE

7. Demonstrate how to use the drawing mode of an integrated package of software to replicate the facade of a building. Special attention should be paid to the geometric shapes and patterns found in the building for easier drawing of the facade. For example, if the front of the house is a square, students use the drawing tool that creates squares. Emphasize the duplication feature in a drawing program to allow for easier repetition of patterns.

8. GROUPING.
   a. INDIVIDUALS.
      Students can work individually to replicate a commercial or industrial building and a residential building.
   b. PAIRS.
      If computers must be shared or if a small-group experience is preferred, students can work in pairs on this project. One student in each pair replicates a commercial or industrial building while the other replicates a residential building. The time needed to complete the computer work depends upon the intricacy of the replicas and the access to computers.

9. After the replicas are completed, encourage students to discuss similarities and differences in their two buildings. This discussion should culminate in a written comparison of the buildings with the original pictures and the printed illustrations attached.

10. Students should select a format for their completed product. Possible products include: a brochure for a realty company, a computer presentation, an oral presentation with overheads, a book, or a poster. Allow class time for students to share their products.

Kingore, B. (1998). Engaging Creative Thinking. Austin: Professional Associates Publishing

NOTES

11. Involve students in evaluating their work. The evaluation form on page 48 was developed to evaluate the work of younger students. The wording on the rubric on page 49 may be more appropriate for secondary students and allows the teacher to weight each criterion. For example, rather than 25 points each, the Product and Content Depth criterion might be weighted as 40 points to indicate its importance to students. When an evaluation form is used as a recorded grade, the team completes their evaluation first. The teacher then uses a different colored pen to evaluate the team on the same sheet. Discussing any differences with the students enhances the learning potential of the evaluation process.

EXTENSIONS FOR STUDENTS

1. VISITING ARCHITECT. Invite an architect to visit the class to demonstrate the tools and blueprints of architecture and to discuss how mathematics and art are connected in architecture. The American Architectural Foundation can connect you to architects in your area.

2. CLASSIFY BUILDINGS. Students make a picture collection or catalog of several interesting buildings and classify them according to their style of architecture, historical period, function, or another category created by the students.

3. LITERATURE. Students enjoy reading fiction works written by David McCauley, an architect and artist. Several of his books such as <u>Cathedral</u> and <u>Unbuilding</u> show various types of structures and are excellent resources for your classroom library during this task. For a humorous alternative, <u>Roberto: The Insect Architect</u> by Nina Laden is a clever book that celebrates creativity and uniqueness in design. Encourage students to identify the famous architects whimsically included in the text.

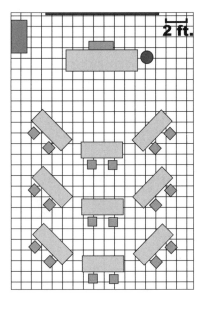

4. GEOMETRY & MEASUREMENT. Students create a floor plan of their classroom or bedroom using graph paper and measurement instruments. Teach the students how to create a scale that will accurately represent the area on the floor plan.

Kingore, B. (1998). <u>Engaging Creative Thinking</u>. Austin: Professional Associates Publishing

5. PANTOMIMING STRUCTURES. Assign each student to research one of the architectural design elements listed on page 43. Then, students interact with other members of the class and form their bodies to represent the structures.

6. SCAVENGER HUNT. Given a list of architectural features, students go on a walking tour taking pictures or sketching the features while recording their locations. Share the results with the class.

7. INDEPENDENT STUDY. Individually or in teams, students study changes in architecture throughout history challenge students to analyze connections between historical events and changes in architecture.

   a. TRENDS ACROSS TIME
      Students compare an architectural style to the trends of that time period and analyze how trends influenced the design of those buildings and later styles.

   b. FAMOUS PEOPLE
      Students research an architect who is considered a leader during a specific period of history. In a written or oral product, students relate the significant events and influences in the architect's life and include visual representations of the work.

   c. ISSUES
      Challenge students to research the most important issues or conflicts affecting architects. What issues relate to different locations?

   d. INVENTIONS
      Students research inventions that have enabled advancements in construction materials and design in architecture.

REFLECTIONS FOR TEACHERS

1. What changes would you make to more effectively allow for students' varying levels of technological ability? How did differing levels of computer skills affect the student pairs?

2. Analyze the thinking skills used in this project.
   • Did students make comparisons easily between two buildings?
   • Did a lack of knowledge of architectural design or architectural terminology limit the students' abilities to make connections and express relationships?
   • Does the final product reflect a gained understanding of architectural design?

Kingore, B. (1998). Engaging Creative Thinking. Austin: Professional Associates Publishing

ARCHITECTURE
TEAM EVALUATION

NAMES _____   DATE _____

Product: 35 total points

___ / _7_ Drawings are clear and precise.
___ / _7_ Evidence of geometric patterns and shapes is present.
___ / _7_ Product includes original picture and computer-drawn replicas.
___ / _7_ Layout of product is aesthetically pleasing.
___ / _7_ Selection of product enhances presentation of material.

Use of Technology: 20 total points

___ / _8_ The drawing tools were used effectively.
___ / _6_ The product was saved and printed properly.
___ / _8_ Word processing enhances the product.

Knowledge and High-Level Thinking: 35 total points

___ / _20_ Analysis of each building shows an understanding of geometric shapes, patterns, and symmetry/asymmetry.
___ / _8_   Comparison of two buildings shows clear understanding of math concepts.
___ / _7_   Knowledge of architectural features is evident in the final product.

Reflection: ___ / 10 points

To work well, I/we _____

_____

_____.

I/We like the way _____

_____

_____.

In the future, I/we would like to _____

_____.

Kingore, B. (1998). Engaging Creative Thinking. Austin: Professional Associates Publishing

ARCHITECTURE
RUBRIC

NAMES _____   DATE _____

CRITERIA	Below passing	70 - 79	80 - 89	90 - 100
Use of Technology Points: / ___	Weak skills; ineffective use of technology ____	Emerging skills; use does not enhance process or product ____	Proficient use of technology; used as a communication tool ____	Advanced use of technology enhances the process and product ____
Planning and Organization Points: / ___	Did not complete plan or lacked a plan ____	Completed with ongoing assistance ____	Completed plan; organized effectively ____	Followed through well; coherent; exceeds expectations ____
Comprehension of Architecture Points: / ___	Comprehension is not demonstrated ____	Response reflects a beginning level of understanding ____	Appropriate use of detail and vocabulary; adequate understanding ____	Precise vocabulary supportive ideas; related concepts; demonstrates thorough understanding ____
Product and Content Depth Points: / ___	Inappropriate product; needs more information or more accurate information ____	Product contains valid content but needs further development or elaboration ____	Analyzes effectively; well developed; explores beyond basic facts and details ____	Precise analysis; in-depth and well-supported; complex concepts and relationships ____
Total Points: / 100	**Comments**			

Kingore, B. (1998). Engaging Creative Thinking. Austin: Professional Associates Publishing

ARCHITECTURE: CONCEPTS AND SKILLS

ART

Connecting art and math to architecture
Constructing meaning and communicating through visual art
Identifying architectural features using visual analysis
Visual layout of information

LANGUAGE ARTS

Comparing and contrasting two structures
Following directions
Oral communication
Written communication

MATH

Identifying and drawing shapes and patterns
Identifying symmetry and asymmetry
Real-world application of mathematical concepts
Measuring and recreating using a scale
Using manipulatives to construct geometric understanding

SOCIAL STUDIES

Accepting individual responsibility
Analyzing structures in relation to time periods in history
Connecting changes in architectural history and the environment
Task commitment
Working in a group

TECH-NOLOGY

Graphic design layout
Using drawing tools
Using technology to construct geometric understanding
Using word processing skills

THINKING SKILLS

Analytical thinking
Classifying
Comparing and Contrasting
Organizing
Planning
Synthesizing
Visual analysis

OTHERS

_____
_____
_____
_____

Kingore, B. (1998). Engaging Creative Thinking. Austin: Professional Associates Publishing

GOLF COURSE

Bertie Kingore

GRADE LEVELS
Fourth through twelfth grade

CONTENT CONNECTION
Language arts, math, science, and social studies

PROBLEM
Students work in teams using trash and recyclable materials to construct one section of a miniature golf course while operating within a budget.

Note: A budget requires more creative thinking since the task must be completed with limited resources. This part of the problem also models the importance of being resourceful.

MATERIALS

1. Masking tape--one roll for each team

2. Scissors--one pair for each student

3. Recyclable materials for construction, e.g., aluminum cans, boxes, cardboard, plastic containers, and newspapers

4. Golf club and golf ball--one for each student

5. Yardstick--one for each team

Kingore, B. (1998). <u>Engaging Creative Thinking</u>. Austin: Professional Associates Publishing

NOTES

Note: Some commercial miniature golf courses lend their golf clubs to a class for a day as a community service and a form of advertising. However, in the spirit of problem solving, it may be more productive for students to create their own golf clubs using dowel rods or yardsticks and recyclable materials. If students bring materials to construct a golf club, those materials are not calculated in the budget.

BACKGROUND

1. ECONOMIC CONCEPTS
   a. Budgets and spread sheets
   b. Fair market value
   c. Supply and demand
   d. Capital
   e. Conservation

2. PHYSICS CONCEPTS
   a. Force--The cause of motion; for every action there is an opposite and equal reaction.
   b. Friction--Surface resistance to relevant motion
   c. Gravity
   d. Inertia--Matter at rest remains at rest; if moving, matter keeps moving in the same direction, unless affected by some outside force.
   e. Reflection--When an object strikes a hard plane obliquely, it rebounds from it, making the angle of reflection equal to the angle of incidence.

3. MATHEMATICAL CONCEPTS
   a. Area
   b. Measurement
   c. Geometry

4. Discuss cooperative learning, team building, and team member roles.

5. Discuss the three R's--reduce, recycle, and reuse. Discuss the kinds of items typically thrown away in daily use which may be recycled or reused.

BUDGET COMMITTEE

Due to the limited capital for this project, construction must be completed for $0.67 or less per hole. Each team submits a budget sheet to the Budget Committee listing each item used, quantity, per unit cost (fair market value), and the total cost. Use the provided Budget Sheet or a computer spread sheet.

Kingore, B. (1998). <u>Engaging Creative Thinking</u>. Austin: Professional Associates Publishing

The Budget Committee is composed of volunteers. Each team may decide to have between zero and two members volunteer to serve on the committee. The teacher serves as chairperson.

CRITERIA

1. Each hole, from tee to fairway, green, and cup, must be designed within a space of three feet by three feet.

   VARIATION FOR OLDER STUDENTS: Each hole, from tee to fairway, green, and cup, must be designed within an area of nine to ten square feet.

2. The hole must be constructed from recyclable or reusable items.

3. Each hole must have barriers to keep the ball contained while in play.

4. While traveling from tee to cup, the ball must encounter a forced change of direction.

5. While traveling from tee to cup, the ball must encounter a forced change in elevation.

6. Each team must devise a cup on the green that will stop and contain the ball.

7. The total construction cost of each hole must not exceed $0.67, as documented by the team's Budget Sheet and approved by the Budget Committee.

8. Each team will have 45 minutes to construct the hole and conduct practice shots.

9. Each team will establish and post the par for that hole. Par may not be less than the lowest score achieved by any team member during practice.

PROCEDURE

FIRST SESSION

BUDGET PREPARATION. Create a class-generated budget reference sheet. Brainstorm and list numerous recyclables that might be used to construct this golf course. Beside each item, research and list the fair market value. For example, what is the current recycle value of a soda can? Encourage resourceful problem solving in determining fair market value. Contact dry cleaners to determine what they pay to buy back wire hangers. Use 800 phone numbers to survey companies regarding the value of their packaging, e.g., plastic bottles, oatmeal cartons, and paper roll tubes.

Kingore, B. (1998). Engaging Creative Thinking. Austin: Professional Associates Publishing

NOTES   Assign students to research and determine the value of the remaining items. Set a schedule for presenting their results to the class.

SECOND SESSION

1. PRICE LISTING. Complete a class budget reference sheet by listing prices beside every item. Some negotiation and group consensus building may be necessary.

2. ASSIGN COOPERATIVE GROUPS. Groups of three or four are preferable to encourage diverse ideas while increasing active participation.

3. TEAM PLANNING. Brainstorm as a team:
   a. What might your part of the golf course look like? Discuss different styles and designs of miniature golf courses you have seen.

   VARIATION FOR OLDER STUDENTS: In what shape might the team design the hole to involve the required area in square feet while creating the greatest challenge for players?

   b. What kind of recyclable or reusable items are needed for this construction?
   c. What recyclable items can each person collect?
   d. What hazards can the team employ to cause the ball to change directions while in motion?
   e. How might a hazard be constructed to change the elevation of the ball while on its path to the cup?
   f. What kinds and quantities of materials for construction can the team afford?
   g. Which team member is responsible for recording budget data and totaling the spread sheet?
   h. Determine which, if any, member(s) of the team will volunteer to serve on the Budget Committee. Discuss the advantages or disadvantages of team members volunteering for this committee.
   i. Submit a design for the score card to be used for student rounds and for the grade level tournament.

4. SCORE CARD. The class collaborates to combine all features of the score card designs to create the class score card.

THIRD SESSION

1. Students bring recyclable materials to school.

2. Students construct golf clubs if they are responsible for making their own.

Kingore, B. (1998). Engaging Creative Thinking. Austin: Professional Associates Publishing

3. Each team measures and uses masking tape to mark off their three foot by three foot section or a nine to ten square foot area.

4. Each team works together to select items from the collected materials brought by that group. All team members must be actively and equally involved in constructing their section of the golf course.

5. Team members may conduct practice shots during the construction phase and make adaptations to increase the complexity and effectiveness of their hole. Discuss angles for banking shots off a barrier.

6. The team completes the budget sheet and submits it to the Budget Committee for review.

7. The Budget Committee approves the budget after asking for changes or clarifications from all teams.

8. Each team member then tees off, plays the hole, and records the score.

9. Team members reach a team consensus to establish par for their hole. Par may not be fewer strokes than the lowest score any team member attained. Post a sign at the tee designating the par.

10. Team members clean their work area.

Note: This section of the task may be divided into two sessions of 20 to 25 minutes each if one 45 minute session is not appropriate for your students or conducive to your schedule.

FOURTH SESSION

1. At each tee, one team member is on hand to answer questions and explain their intended procedure.

2. Allow time for students to play a round of miniature golf and record their scores.

3. EVALUATION. Each team collaborates to complete an evaluation form. The evaluation is intended as a metacognitive response for group awareness, but it can be a recorded grade. When used as a recorded grade, the team should collaboratively complete their evaluation first; then, the teacher evaluates the team on the same sheet. Discussing any differences with the students enhances the learning potential of the evaluation process.

Kingore, B. (1998). Engaging Creative Thinking. Austin: Professional Associates Publishing

NOTES

LATER

When interest in the completed course wanes, each team takes apart their section and sorts each item according to its recyclable category. Arrange for the items to be delivered to a recycling container or center.

EXTENSIONS FOR STUDENTS

1. Students create a blueprint before constructing their course. Compare the plan to the completed structure.

2. Construct the golf course outside. What kinds of trash and recyclable materials are weather safe and more appropriate to use for this construction? Arrange permission for the students to play the course after school.

3. Arrange to set up the course in a children's ward of a local hospital or senior citizens home for one day as a special entertainment. Adjust the degree of difficulty to make it appropriate for that population.

4. Encourage computer skills by requiring that the budget sheet be developed on a spread sheet.

5. Allow several classes to contribute two or three of their most difficult holes to create a grade level "challenge course." Arrange for the construction in a multipurpose room or gym. In the spirit of camaraderie, integrate students from different classes to play on the same team.

6. Organize a school-wide golf tournament at the challenge course. Invite the school administrators, faculty, and staff to participate.

YOU ARE INVITED TO PARTICIPATE IN THE 8TH GRADE
PRO/AM RECYCLABLE GOLF TOURNAMENT.

Wednesday, October 23   9:45 a.m.   Scott Multipurpose Room

ENTRY FEE: One non-perishable item to be donated to the Humble Children's Shelter

 Refreshments will be served in the players' tent
at the conclusion of the tournament.

Determine different kinds of entry fees that could be collected to benefit others. Some possibilities include: non-perishable food for a shelter, animal food or toys to donate to the animal shelter, toys for a local children's home, or toiletries for homeless families. Also, have each class or team prepare a food or a drink to serve as refreshments during the tournament.

Kingore, B. (1998). Engaging Creative Thinking. Austin: Professional Associates Publishing

GOLF COURSE: STUDENT COPY
Bertie Kingore

PROBLEM

Students work in teams using trash and recyclable materials to construct one section of a miniature golf course while operating within a budget.

MATERIALS

1. Masking tape--one roll for each team
2. Scissors--one pair for each student
3. Recyclable trash for construction materials,
   e.g., aluminum cans, boxes, cardboard, plastic containers, and newspapers
4. Golf club and golf ball--one for each student
5. Yardstick--one for each team

BUDGET COMMITTEE

Due to the limited capital for this project, construction must be completed for $0.67 or less per hole. Each team must submit a Budget Sheet to the Budget Committee listing each item used, quantity, per unit cost (fair market value) and the total. Use the Budget Sheet provided, or create a spread sheet completed on a computer.

The Budget Committee is composed of volunteers. Each team may decide to have between zero and two members volunteer to serve on the Committee. The teacher serves as chairperson.

CRITERIA

1. Each hole, from tee to fairway, green, and cup, must be designed within a space of three feet by three feet.
   Variation for older students: Each hole, from tee to fairway, green, and cup, must be designed within an area of nine to ten square feet.
2. The hole must be constructed from recyclable or reusable items.
3. Each hole must have barriers to keep the ball contained while in play.
4. While traveling from tee to the cup, the ball must encounter a forced change of direction.
5. While traveling from tee to the cup, the ball must encounter a forced change in elevation.
6. Each team must devise a cup on the green that will stop and contain the ball.
7. The total construction cost of each hole must not exceed $0.67, as documented by the team's Budget Sheet and approved by the Budget Committee.

Kingore, B. (1998). Engaging Creative Thinking. Austin: Professional Associates Publishing

8. Each team will have 45 minutes to construct the hole and conduct practice shots.
9. Each team will establish and post the par for that hole. Par may not be less than the lowest score made by any team member during practice.

TEAM PLANNING

Brainstorm as a team:

1. What might your part of the golf course look like? Discuss different styles and designs of miniature golf courses you have seen.
    Variation for older students: In what shape might the team design the hole to involve the required area in square feet while creating the greatest challenge for players?
2. What kind of recyclable or reusable items are needed for this construction?
3. What recyclable items can each person collect?
4. What hazards can cause the ball to change directions while in motion?
5. How might a hazard be constructed to change the elevation of the ball while on its path to the cup?
6. What kinds and quantities of construction materials can the team afford?
7. Which team member is responsible for recording budget data and totaling the spread sheet?
8. Determine which, if any, member(s) of your team will volunteer to serve on the Budget Committee. Discuss the advantages or disadvantages of team members serving on this committee.
9. Submit a design for the score card to be used for student rounds and for the tournament.

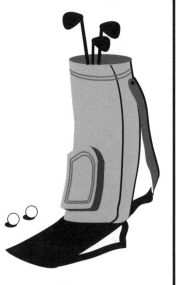

TEAM CONSTRUCTION

1. Measure and then use masking tape to mark a three by three feet section or an area totaling nine to ten square feet.
2. Work together to select items from your collected materials. All team members must be actively and equally involved in constructing your section of the golf course.
3. Conduct practice shots during the construction phase, making adaptations to increase the complexity and effectiveness of the hole. Discuss angles for banking shots off of a barrier.
4. Complete your budget sheet and submit it to the Budget Committee for review.
5. Each team member then tees off, plays the hole, and records the score.
6. Reach a team consensus to establish par for the hole. Par may not be fewer strokes than the lowest score attained by any team member during practice. Create a sign stating par for the hole, and post it at the tee.
7. Clean your work area.
8. After playing the entire course, collaborate to complete an Evaluation form.

Kingore, B. (1998). <u>Engaging Creative Thinking</u>. Austin: Professional Associates Publishing

GOLF COURSE
BUDGET SHEET

NAME _____   DATE _____

Items used in your course:	Quantity	Fair Market Value	Subtotal

TOTAL	**$**
Budget	**$ 0.67**
Difference	**$**

❏ Budget is under: $_____

❏ Budget is over: $_____

Kingore, B. (1998). <u>Engaging Creative Thinking</u>. Austin: Professional Associates Publishing

GOLF COURSE
EVALUATION

NAME _____ DATE _____

AS A TEAM WE:	😞 No	😐 OK	🙂 Good	😀 Great
Stayed on task.				
Met the required criteria.				
Helped each other problem solve.				
Negotiated differences.				
Tried creative ideas.				
Worked within our budget.				
Worked quietly together.				
Encouraged each other.				

Our team worked well together because _____

_____

_____.

One thing we particularly liked is _____

_____

_____.

One thing we would do differently is _____

_____

_____.

We want others to know _____

_____

_____.

Kingore, B. (1998). Engaging Creative Thinking. Austin: Professional Associates Publishing

GOLF COURSE
EVALUATION

NAMES _____ DATE _____

1. Draw and label a diagram of your section of the course to explain how your design used the required area while creating the greatest challenge for players. (25 points)

2. Explain how each of the following science concepts is demonstrated in the design, construction, or playing of your section of the golf course. (5 points each)

Deflection: _____

_____

_____

Inertia: _____

_____

_____

Friction: _____

_____

_____

Force: _____

_____

_____

Gravity: _____

_____

_____

3. Draw a diagram of the most difficult parts of the course. Analyze what makes those sections more complex and label the scientific principles demonstrated? (25 points)

4. What would you change or add to your course if your budget was larger? (25 points)

Kingore, B. (1998). Engaging Creative Thinking. Austin: Professional Associates Publishing

GOLF COURSE: CONCEPTS AND SKILLS

LANGUAGE ARTS
Classifying similarities and/or differences
Listening to instructions and listening to others
Oral communication
Reading and following directions
Vocabulary development
Writing for a variety of purposes

MATH
Calculating area
Geometric shapes
Measurement/measurement tools
Spread sheet

SCIENCE
Classifying objects from the environment
Ecology
Force
Friction
Gravity
Inertia
Deflection

SOCIAL STUDIES
Accepting responsibility
Compromising
Building consensus
Group cooperation
Standards of honesty and fairness
Task commitment

THINKING SKILLS
Analytical thinking
Comparing and contrasting
Evaluation
Planning
Organizing
Synthesizing

OTHERS
_____
_____
_____
_____
_____
_____

Kingore, B. (1998). <u>Engaging Creative Thinking</u>. Austin: Professional Associates Publishing

ROAD RALLY

Kathy Hall

GRADE LEVELS
Fourth through twelfth grade

CONTENT CONNECTION
Language arts, math, science, and social studies

PROBLEM
Students work in groups to design and construct a self-propelled vehicle using materials the team "purchases" with allotted money.

MATERIALS AND PRICES

CONSTRUCTION ITEMS	PRICE
1. One-half of a piece of poster board or two file folders	$5.00
2. Three sheets of paper	2.00
3. Two rubber bands	15.00
4. One balloon	15.00
5. Three plastic soda straws	2.00
6. Two yards of masking tape	1.00
7. Two pencils	3.00
8. One empty paper towel roll	Free, but provide your own

Kingore, B. (1998). <u>Engaging Creative Thinking</u>. Austin: Professional Associates Publishing

NOTES

MANUFACTURING ITEMS (Items used to create the vehicle but not as a part of the vehicle)	PRICE
1. Scissors	1.00
2. Compass	1.00
3. Pen or pencil for writing only	Free

BACKGROUND

Basic physics concepts which may be taught through this activity are:

- Friction--the force that resists relative motion between two bodies in contact;
- Inertia--a property of matter by which it remains at rest or in uniform motion in a straight line unless acted upon by some external force;
- Kinetic Energy--the energy a body has by virtue of being in motion; and
- Potential Energy--the energy a body has due to its configuration.

TEST SITE

The testing area for vehicles needs to be no more than a three by four foot space on your classroom floor. Some students feel strongly that their vehicle will run better on carpet, and some like a slick surface. By setting up two sites, both preferences can be accommodated.

Use masking tape to mark the starting line. Make a masking tape finish line two feet from the beginning, or have a yard stick or other measuring device handy to measure the distance that each vehicle travels. (Sometimes "traveling in a straight line" will have to be broadly interpreted.) Vehicles are placed at the starting line and must travel two feet. Allow students to use the test site for pretesting their vehicles during assembly. The Pit Stop Authority, i.e., teacher or person designated by the teacher, oversees the official tests.

A space on a table or desk should be cleared for students to display their completed vehicles. Use an index card to number each vehicle in the display.

EXAMPLES OF SUCCESSFUL VEHICLES

Although one of the joys of this activity is watching students generate unexpectedly effective ideas to meet the criteria, it is desirable to have a few ideas handy to assist groups who are truly stuck. Directions for three of the most popular styles follow.

Kingore, B. (1998). Engaging Creative Thinking. Austin: Professional Associates Publishing

1. THE SLED. This is a sleigh-like vehicle which moves on straw runners (optional) and is powered by a balloon on top of the vehicle. The body is usually made of paper or tag board, and everything is held together with tape. Students blow the balloon up before the test and release it when the test begins. The air escaping from the balloon powers the vehicle forward. One problem with this prototype is finding the proper weight. The vehicle must be light enough to move easily yet heavy enough to prevent blowing over or running off course. The testing surface must be smooth, because friction is the enemy of the sled style. The sled is not easy to propel in a straight line, but students can conquer this challenge.

2. THE CHARIOT-LESS CHARIOT. This is a one-axled, two wheeled vehicle with no body. The wheels are cut from tag board and attached to a straw or pencil axle with masking tape. A free spinning ring made of masking tape circles the axle. A balloon is attached to this ring. When the blown-up balloon is released the air pushes the vehicle forward. This vehicle performs well as long as the wheels are the same size and the ring is an equal distance from both wheels. This vehicle runs best with a little traction but can work on a smooth surface.

3. THE RUBBER-BAND WAGON. This vehicle is a true two-axled, four wheeled car. The body and wheels are usually made of tag board. Two pencils serve as axles, which stick out through holes in the body of the car. The axles are stuck through the four tag board wheels. A rubber band is stretched between the front and back axles, attached to both with masking tape and then wound around the back axle until there is considerable tension. When the rubber band is released, the axle spins and the vehicle moves. Problems with the vehicle are keeping the wheels even and the vehicle light enough to move. This vehicle works better on a slightly rough surface.

EVALUATIONS

The two evaluations for this task offer teachers a choice, depending on the objectives emphasized in the activity. While the initial section of both evaluations assess how closely the vehicle meets the construction standards, the first evaluation calls for a more holistic appraisal, while the second calls for more detailed analysis. The last sections of the two evaluations are very different. The first evaluation looks at the group process and cooperation during the construction; the second evaluation stresses science concepts as applied to the movement of the vehicle.

Kingore, B. (1998). Engaging Creative Thinking. Austin: Professional Associates Publishing

NOTES

The evaluations are intended as metacognitive responses for group awareness, but they may be used as recorded grades. When used as a recorded grade, the individual or team completes the evaluation first. The teacher then makes a final appraisal on the same sheet. Discussing any differences with the students enhances the learning potential of the evaluation process.

BACKGROUND FOR STUDENTS

Students can begin with little background as this challenge is intended to be an exploratory physics activity.

1. MATHEMATICAL CONCEPTS.
   a. Conversion of data to percentages
   b. Budgeting
   c. Scale

2. PHYSICS CONCEPTS.
   a. Potential energy--the energy a body has due to its configuration
   b. Kinetic energy--the energy a body has by virtue of being in motion
   c. Inertia--a property of matter by which it remains at rest or in uniform motion in a straight line unless acted upon by some external force
   d. Friction--the force that resists relative motion between two bodies in contact; surface resistance to relative motion

3. Discuss group dynamics, shared authority, and team building.

CRITERIA

1. Each team must construct a vehicle.

2. It must start from a stand-still and move at least two feet in a straight line on a level surface under its own power.

3. Each team has $26.00 to spend on materials. Only materials on the list are to be used in construction. Teams purchase items on the list of materials from the Pit Stop Authority. Throughout the problem, they may purchase additional materials from the list if they have the money.

4. The official testing area and testing procedures are under the control of the Pit Stop Authority who may make any rules necessary to preserve the spirit of this challenge.

5. Construction teams have 30 minutes planning time and 30 minutes to assemble and pretest their vehicles.

Kingore, B. (1998). <u>Engaging Creative Thinking</u>. Austin: Professional Associates Publishing

PROCEDURE

1. PLANNING (30 minutes)
    a. Assign groups of three or four. Place students with strong mechanical abilities in different groups to equalize opportunities for success.
    b. Introduce the activity and the criteria for success.
    c. Point out to the teams that they lack sufficient money to buy all of the listed construction materials and manufacturing equipment. Encourage them to use materials carefully as no replacements can be provided.
    d. Advise teams to brainstorm ideas and concur on a design for their vehicle. Some brainstorming prompts are:
        •   What are the attributes of a vehicle?
        •   What are the attributes of a self-propelled vehicle?
        •   What are different ways to make an object move across the floor?
        •   Which materials will produce power?
        •   How can you use these materials to produce power?
        •   Can you purchase these materials with the money allotted?
        •   Are there ways to save money?

2. CONSTRUCTING (30 minutes)
    a. Distribute money sheets to each team, and ask students to cut out their allotted currency. (Collect the scissors and extra currency when finished.)
    b. Each team selects one representative to purchase all of the materials and equipment needed by the team. (If teams think of sharing materials and equipment, congratulate them on their problem-solving abilities, remind them that each team must create its own vehicle, and allow the teams to cooperate as much as the rules permit.)
    c. All members of the team assemble the vehicle, pretest it in the testing area as necessary, and clean their work area. Display the vehicles in a designated area.

3. PREDICTING. Using observation and analysis (no touching), each team examines all other vehicles and predicts how far each will travel. On the Performance Prediction worksheet, one member records the team's predictions for each vehicle.

4. VEHICLE PERFORMANCE TESTING. Each team conducts its vehicle's performance run in the designated testing area. The Pit Stop Authority measures the distance each vehicle travels. The teams record the results of each performance on the prediction sheets.

Kingore, B. (1998). Engaging Creative Thinking. Austin: Professional Associates Publishing

NOTES

5. PERCENTAGES
    a. Prediction Percentage. Each team computes the Prediction Percentage by dividing the actual distance traveled by the predicted distance.
    b. Task Percentage. Each team computes the task percentage by dividing the actual distance traveled by the required distance.

6. DEBRIEFING. Conduct a class discussion about the results of the vehicle tests. Some possible questions are:
    *   What was your greatest difficulty in assembling the vehicle? How did you overcome it?
    *   Did you need more time, money, or types of materials?
    *   Which vehicle did you think would go farthest? Why?
    *   Which vehicle surprised you the most? Why?
    *   Why did some vehicles move erratically? What corrections could be made?
    *   Which vehicle had the most energy? How do you know?
    *   Which vehicle had the greatest inertia? How do you know?
    *   Which vehicle was best designed to overcome air resistance?
    *   How did friction affect different vehicles?
    *   Which vehicle do you admire the most? Why?

7. AUTO SHOW. Leave the vehicles on display for extension activities or further testing. Take photographs as momentoes.

8. EVALUATION. Either of the evaluation forms may be completed by teams or individual students.

9. LATER. When the class loses interest in the completed vehicles, have each team disassemble its vehicle and return reusable items (unbroken pencils or straws, rubber bands) to the classroom supplies. Consider using the play money from this construction problem as "refunds" to students returning materials. Perhaps serious recyclers could use accumulated money to buy a homework pass later on!

EXTENSIONS FOR STUDENTS

1. VARIATIONS
    a. Eliminate material costs.
    b. Require the vehicle to travel uphill for one foot. Prop up a board for a test track.
    c. Require the vehicle to carry a film canister with a designated number of pennies inside.
    d. Require the vehicle to travel in a circular pattern.

Kingore, B. (1998). Engaging Creative Thinking. Austin: Professional Associates Publishing

**Sleek
Propulsion in an
Extraordinarily
Energized
Dragster**

2. ACRONYM NAME. Teams brainstorm words associated with cars or racing. They choose one word to use as a name for their vehicle and develop an acronym for that name. Students label their vehicle with their acronym and challenge other students to guess its meaning.

3. RALLY ROUTE. Tell students that the three to four feet of the test area is the real-world equivalent of three to four miles. Students refer to atlases, road maps, and other resources to plan a real-world route for the vehicles. They create a scale model of the route using butcher paper, markers, and recycled boxes to represent buildings or terrain along the route. Challenge older students to determine the real-world distance they traveled using the percent of scale-model distance they traveled.

4. ATTRIBUTE LISTING. Teams brainstorm and list characteristics of their car, including quantitative and elaborated observations about the car.

5. ODE TO A FLIMSY CAR. Using the attribute list generated in the previous activity, each student composes a poem of praise to the team's vehicle.

6. GLOBAL PARADE. Assign each group a country to research. The class brainstorms a list of questions regarding driving. (How many people drive? How many people own a car? Do cars drive on the left or right side of the road? How much does gas cost? What are the most popular models of cars?) Students research the answers for their assigned country. The results are displayed on a bulletin board. For additional challenge, students learn the names of some parts of cars in the language of their assigned country. They demonstrate their knowledge using their vehicle as a visual aid.

7. SPONSORS. Just as professional race cars are decorated with the logos of sponsors (Pennzoil™, GM™, Midas Muffler™), students' vehicles can have sponsors who want to advertise their products. Students design logos and slogans for imaginary sponsors to decorate their vehicles. (For example: "Acme Rubber. We put the S–T–R–E–T–C–H in limos!")

8. DREAM MACHINE. Based on their experiences in designing a car and their observations of other designs, students draw and label all parts of an improved vehicle that meets the same criteria but may use any additional materials readily found in the classroom.

9. "HOW IT ALL BEGAN." Students write a narrative that begins: "I could not believe my eyes. There it was..." or "I thought it was an impossible task! We were told..." The story ends with the vehicle test in the classroom.

Kingore, B. (1998). Engaging Creative Thinking. Austin: Professional Associates Publishing

ROAD RALLY: STUDENT COPY
Kathy Hall

PROBLEM

Students work in groups to design and construct a self-propelled vehicle using materials the team "purchases" with allotted money.

MATERIALS AND PRICES

CONSTRUCTION ITEMS	PRICE
1. One-half sheet of poster board or two file folders	$5.00
2. Three sheets of paper	2.00
3. Two rubber bands	15.00
4. One balloon	15.00
5. Three plastic soda straws	2.00
6. Two yards of masking tape	1.00
7. Two pencils	3.00
8. One empty paper towel roll	Free, but provide your own

MANUFACTURING ITEMS (Items used to create the vehicle but not as a part of the vehicle)	PRICE
1. Scissors	1.00
2. Compass	1.00
3. Pen or pencil for writing only	Free

CRITERIA

1. Each team must construct a vehicle.

2. It must start from a stand-still and move at least two feet in a straight line on a level surface under its own power.

3. Your team has $26.00 to spend on materials. Only materials on the list may be used in construction. You purchase items on the list of materials from the Pit Stop Authority. Throughout the problem, you may purchase additional materials from the list if your team has the money to pay for them.

Kingore, B. (1998). <u>Engaging Creative Thinking</u>. Austin: Professional Associates Publishing

4. The official testing area and procedures are under the control of the Pit Stop Authority who may change any rules necessary to preserve the spirit of this challenge.

5. Your team has 30 minutes planning time and 30 minutes assembly and pretesting time.

PROCEDURE

1. PLANNING (30 minutes)
   a. Your team lacks sufficient money to buy all of the listed construction materials and manufacturing equipment. Use purchased materials carefully as no replacements are provided.
   b. Brainstorm ideas, and concur on a design for your vehicle. Some brainstorming prompts are:
      • What are the attributes of a vehicle?
      • What are the attributes of a self-propelled vehicle?
      • What are different ways to make an object move across the floor?
      • Which materials will produce power?
      • How can you use these materials to produce power?
      • Can you purchase these materials with the amount of money given?
      • Are there ways to save money?

2. CONSTRUCTING (30 minutes)
   a. Cut out your allotted currency, and return the scissors and extra currency to your teacher.
   b. Select one representative to purchase materials and equipment.
   c. Work together to assemble the vehicle, pre-test it in the testing area as necessary, and clean your work area. Display your completed vehicle in the designated area.

3. PREDICTING. Using only observation and analysis (no touching), examine all other vehicles, and predict the distance each will travel. On the Performance Predictions worksheet, record your team's predictions for each vehicle.

4. VEHICLE PERFORMANCE TESTING. Conduct your vehicle's performance run in the designated testing area. The Pit Stop Authority measures the distance your vehicle travels, and you record the results on your team's Performance Predictions sheet.

5. PERCENTAGES
   a. Prediction Percentage. Each team computes the prediction percentage by dividing the actual distance traveled by the predicted distance.
   b. Task Percentage. Each team computes the task percentage by dividing the actual distance traveled by the required distance.

6. EVALUATION. The evaluation forms are completed by the team or individual students.

Kingore, B. (1998). Engaging Creative Thinking. Austin: Professional Associates Publishing

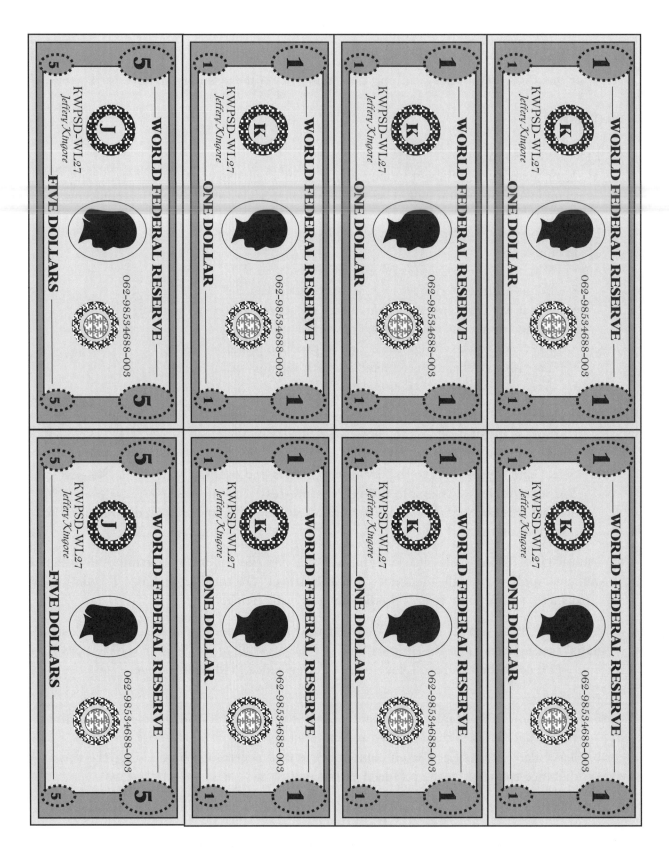

Kingore, B. (1998). <u>Engaging Creative Thinking</u>. Austin: Professional Associates Publishing

ROAD RALLY CHALLENGE
PERFORMANCE PREDICTIONS

NAME _____ DATE _____

Group	What gives it power?	How far will it travel?	How far did it travel?	Prediction Percentage	Task Percentage
Ex.	balloon	3.0 feet	2.2 feet	73%	110%
1.					
2.					
3.					
4.					
5.					
6.					
7.					
8.					
9.					
10.					
11.					
12.					
13.					
14.					

Kingore, B. (1998). Engaging Creative Thinking. Austin: Professional Associates Publishing

ROAD RALLY CHALLENGE
EVALUATION

NAMES_____   DATE _____

Construction: 30 total points

____ / 10   We constructed our own vehicle according to our plan and design.

____ / 10   Our vehicle traveled at least two feet under its own power.

____ / 10   We spent $26.00 or less on materials.

Cooperation: 40 total points

____ / 10   We all contributed ideas to our design. Explain how.
              _____
              _____

____ / 10   We all agreed on a final plan and design for our vehicle. Explain how.
              _____
              _____

____ / 10   We all helped in constructing the vehicle by _____
              _____
              _____ .

____ / 10   We all worked at the less fun parts (clean up, getting materials, etc.).
              Explain how. _____
              _____

Learning: 10 points each (list on another paper)

•   Things we learned about self-propulsion
•   Things we learned about prediction
•   Things we learned about percentages

Suggestion:

Next time, we _____

_____

Kingore, B. (1998). Engaging Creative Thinking. Austin: Professional Associates Publishing

ROAD RALLY CHALLENGE
EVALUATION

NAMES _____   DATE _____

Construction Requirements: 50 total points

____ / 16   The construction qualifies as a vehicle.

Definition of vehicle: _____

_____

Source of definition: _____

How does your construction match the definition? _____

_____

_____

____ / 16   The construction is self-propelled.

Definition of self-propelled. _____

_____

Source of definition: _____

How did your vehicle's performance match the definition? _____

_____

_____

____ / 6   The construction traveled at least two feet.

____ / 6   The construction traveled in a straight line.

____ / 6   Materials cost $26.00 or less.

Scientific Concepts: 50 total points

____ / 25   Draw a detailed diagram of your vehicle. Label your drawing with the following concepts: air resistance, friction, inertia, potential energy, and kinetic energy.

____ / 25   Explain how each affects your vehicle.

Kingore, B. (1998). Engaging Creative Thinking. Austin: Professional Associates Publishing

ROAD RALLY: CONCEPTS AND SKILLS

LANGUAGE ARTS
Listening to instructions and listening to others
Oral communication
Writing for a variety of purposes
Description

MATH
Calculating distance
Converting data into percentages
Proportions and ratios

SCIENCE
Developing and testing hypotheses
Air resistance
Friction
Inertia
Investigating models
Kinetic and potential energy

SOCIAL STUDIES
Accepting responsibility
Compromising and building consensus
Economics of limited resources
Group cooperation
Learning about other cultures
Map making
Standards of honesty and fairness
Supply and demand
Task commitment

THINKING SKILLS
Analytical thinking: comparing and contrasting;
    planning; organizing
Designing
Evaluation
Observing
Problem solving
Synthesizing

OTHERS
_____
_____
_____
_____

Kingore, B. (1998). Engaging Creative Thinking. Austin: Professional Associates Publishing

LITTLE GIFTS _____
Jeffery Kingore

School bell.

Uncertain eyes
brave a new classroom
of bubble-gum-breath boys and girls.
With hands in pockets,
a deer in an open field,
I set course to the corner desk.

Strange voices,
oblivious to "the new kid," engulf me.
From the head of the room
comes a soft smile of comfort,
a welcome mat of warmth.

You denied me solitude
with an introduction
and never let go of my hand.
Listening as you taught,
you asked for my thoughts
and fueled originality.
The problems were mine to solve
in your embrace of encouragement,
and learning was a discovery,
a frolic through fields
of imagination.
You taught me to think
with a sword of ideas
and assurance as my shield.

Thank you
for these little gifts
you never knew you gave.

Kingore, B. (1998). Engaging Creative Thinking. Austin: Professional Associates Publishing

REFERENCES

Apollo 13. (1995). A Ron Howard Film. Universal City, CA: Universal City Studios.

Gympel, J. (1996). The Story of Architecture: From Antiquity to the Present. Köln: Könemann.

Isaksen, S. & Treffinger, D. (1985). Creative Problem Solving: The Basic Course. Buffalo, NY: Bearly Ltd.

Kingore, B. (1999). Assessment: Time Saving Procedures for Busy Teachers, 2nd ed. Austin: Professional Associates Publishing.

Kingore, B. (2001). Kingore Observation Inventory, 2nd ed. Austin: Professional Associates Publishing.

Laden, N. (2000). Roberto: The Insect Architect. San Francisco: Chronicle Books.

Macaulay, D. (1980). Unbuilding. New York: Houghton Mifflin. (1973). Cathedral: The Story of Its Construction. New York: Trumpet.

Osborn, A. (1963). Applied Imagination, 3rd ed. New York: Scribner's.

Parnes, S. (1981). Magic of Your Mind. Buffalo, NY: Bearly Ltd.

Payne, R. (1995). Poverty: A Framework for Understanding and Working with Students and Adults from Poverty. Baytown, TX: RFT Publishing.

Tryon, L. (1991). Albert's Alphabet. New York: Aladdin.

Vos Savant, M. (1997). "Ask Marilyn." Parade Magazine, August 10, 1997; 5.

Wilkins, D., Schultz, B., and Linduff, K. (1994). Art Past, Art Present, 2nd ed. New York: Prentice Hall, Inc.